"All are alike unto God"

"All are alike unto God"

EDITED BY
E. DALE LeBARON

Bookcraft
Salt Lake City, Utah

Copyright © 1990 by Bookcraft, Inc.

All rights reserved. No part of this book may be reproduced in any form or by any means without permission in writing from the publisher, Bookcraft, Inc., 1848 West 2300 South, Salt Lake City, Utah 84119.

Bookcraft is a registered trademark of Bookcraft, Inc.

Library of Congress Catalog Card Number: 90-81495

ISBN 0-88494-738-6

First Printing, 1990

Printed in the United States of America

For [God] doeth that which is good among the children of men; . . . and he inviteth them all to come unto him and partake of his goodness; and he denieth none that come unto him, black and white, bond and free, male and female; . . . and all are alike unto God.

—2 Nephi 26:33

Contents

	Preface	ix
	Acknowledgments	xi
	Introduction	1
	GHANA	
1	*Joseph William Billy Johnson* We Felt the Spirit of the Pioneers	13
2	*Emmanuel Abu Kissi* I Have Found the Fulness	24
3	*Priscilla Sampson-Davis* An Instrument in His Hands	36
4	*Joseph Kwamena Otoo* I Was Persecuted for My Faith	43
	NIGERIA	
5	*David William Eka* Growing with the Church	55
6	*Faustina Aba Haizel* The Church Has Touched My Life, Polishing My Whole Being	65
7	*Stephen C. Ejielo* Seek First the Kingdom, Then Retain the Spirit	73
8	*Florence N. Chukwurah* I Had Peace. . . . A Spiritual Satisfaction	80
9	*Celestine N. Onuka* Nothing Good Comes Easy	88

| 10 | *Jude I. Inmpey*
The Lord's Hands Upon Me .... | 95 |

ZAIRE

| 11 | *Baende L. E. I. Isekuncola*
I Had Been Searching for God .... | 105 |
| 12 | *Mbuyi Nkitabungi*
Something Touched Me ... It Was the Spirit .... | 110 |

ZIMBABWE

13	*Adjei Kwame* Now I Was at Home	119
14	*Ernest Sibanda* I Am a Free Man	125
15	*Sabbath Sibanda Maturure* Only God Knows Our Problems	133

SOUTH AFRICA

16	*Julia N. Mavimbela* Where There Has Been a Bloodstain, a Beautiful Flower Must Grow	141
17	*Moses Mahlangu* I Waited Fourteen Years	153
18	*Erna Raikes* Live in Harmony, Despite Differences	162
19	*Dolly Henrietta Ndhlovu* Come and Follow Jesus Christ	169
20	*Alice Johanna Okkers* I Would Love to Touch the Door of the Temple.........	176
21	*Sello Isaac Mbele* I Began to Feel Loved............................	181
22	*Elias M. Vis, Sr.* A New Life and a New Covenant— Bring Peace and Harmony to Our Land	187
23	*Ella Volenhoven* Now I Realize ... What I Am Worth	197

Preface

This book is a selection of twenty-three conversion stories by black African Latter-day Saints, as related and recorded from May to August 1988. These converts are from the five African countries which were the first to receive Latter-day Saint missionaries: South Africa, Zimbabwe, Nigeria, Ghana, and Zaire. The body of oral histories from which these few were selected consisted of some four hundred interviews and represented more than four hundred hours of recordings.

The English of the informants, often their second language, posed a challenge to the transcribers, who simply tried their best to remain faithful to the language and intent of the interviewees while working to achieve readability. In the process of editing the narratives for this book efforts similarly were made to retain the authentic voices of the interviewees, their language being changed only to the extent necessary to assure clarity. Thus, while continuity has been created by the omission of the interviewer's questions and often by rearranging the interview, the words of the narrators remain essentially theirs.

As the acknowledgments indicate, many have provided assistance at various stages of the work, and to them all I express my appreciation. I am above all grateful for the hundreds of African people who accepted the message of the restored gospel—often at great personal sacrifice—and for their willingness to share their conversion stories with their brothers and sisters in the gospel.

Acknowledgments

Deep appreciation is expressed to the David M. Kennedy Center for International Studies and to the Department of Church History and Doctrine at Brigham Young University, who from beginning to end were supportive and helpful to the oral history project in Africa.

Valuable assistance was provided by many during the preparation phase of the project: Elder Alexander Morrison of the United Kingdom/Ireland/Africa Area Presidency; Spencer J. Palmer and Roger Keller of the David M. Kennedy Center for International Studies; Wes and Mariane Johnson from the BYU History Department; Glen G. Fisher, and other former mission presidents in Africa; and numerous others.

The following mission presidents and wives made the work in Africa possible and productive: President and Sister Miles Cunningham (Ghana); President and Sister Robert Sackley (Nigeria); President and Sister Bay Hutchings (Zaire); President and Sister Joseph Hamstead (Zimbabwe); President and Sister R. J. Snow and President and Sister Reed Snow (South Africa). In South Africa, valuable help was provided also by Don Harper, Regional Representative for South Africa, and President Anthony Courtney of the Durban Natal Stake presidency. In addition, throughout the five countries many wonderful mission couples, missionaries, and local members made significant contributions to the quality of the project.

The hundreds of interviews were transcribed by BYU students: Rachel Huber (who transcribed more than half of the interviews); Bill George; Amy Olsen; Dee Henderson; Karin Harman; and Jana-Lyn Dursteler. Curtis LeBaron assisted with the editing.

I express heartfelt appreciation to those named above and also to those who can be mentioned only in general terms.

I express special gratitude to my wife, Laura, and to our children and their spouses: Debra and Keri St. Jeor; Angela and Curtis Cummings; Curtis and Jan LeBaron; Rachel and Steve Huber; Shawna and Clark Hammond; our son David LeBaron; and our eleven grandchildren. The family members' love, faith, prayers, and letters sustained me during the long 101 days in Africa.

I express particular thanks to Don Norton for the enormous help he gave by his skillful editing of about two-thirds of the transcribed narratives used to produce this book; for his cooperative spirit and attitude exhibited throughout the editing process generally; and for the patience and support of Don's wife, Gloria, who, being herself a convert to the restored gospel, took a special interest in this project. I am also grateful to the College of Humanities, BYU, for the released time they granted Don to do the editing work.

Introduction

The declaration of The Church of Jesus Christ of Latter-day Saints that we believe God "will yet reveal many great and important things pertaining to the Kingdom of God" is powerfully verified by the revelation extending the priesthood to all worthy male members and temple blessings to all worthy members of the Church. Regarding the significance of this revelation of 1 June 1978, President Kimball endorsed the statement that it brought "one of the greatest changes and blessings that has ever been known" (Spencer W. Kimball, *The Teachings of Spencer W. Kimball*, Edward L. Kimball, ed. [Salt Lake City: Bookcraft, 1982], p. 451). In terms of its impact, this revelation must be one of the greatest ever received. It opened the door for all temple ordinances to be performed for all people back to the beginning of history. This revelation is a vital part of the restitution of all things in preparation for the mission of the millennial era.

I was presiding over the South Africa Johannesburg Mission at the time when the priesthood and temple blessings were extended to all worthy male members of the Church. Because there were no black male members of the Church in that mission, the revelation had no immediate effect on members. But it was obvious that in the days ahead it would perhaps have a greater impact on Africa than on any other part of the world.

Just before the revelation was announced, I had received requests for information about the Church from black people in southern Africa. These inquiries greatly increased after June 1978, even though very few of the inquirers knew anything of the revelation. The Lord had poured out his Spirit on the blacks of Africa, just as he had inspired the prophet.

The blacks, being much more given to speaking than to writing, are unaccustomed to keeping written records. That fact, along with my concern that time might rob us of valuable histories of early black converts, led me to propose an oral history project to the ten countries where the Church was established in Africa a decade after the 1978 revelation—South Africa, Zimbabwe, Ghana, Nigeria, Zaire, Ciskei, Transkei, Swaziland, and the island nations of Mauritius and Reunion. My concern was verified when Violet Dube, a pioneer saint in Soweto, South Africa, passed away just two weeks after I had interviewed her in the Johannesburg Temple. Her story is the only record of her great life.

The opportunity to collect oral histories from African Saints came in 1988, when the David M. Kennedy Center for International Studies at Brigham Young University approved funding for me to travel to Africa for that purpose. Mission presidents throughout Africa helped in any way they could. I seemed to receive help from the Lord too—the favorable timing of many interviews was remarkable, for instance. Experienced collectors of oral history told me that I would be fortunate to average one interview a day in Africa, but on some days I did as many as a dozen, and in one hundred days I accumulated more than four hundred interviews!

A Brief History of the Church in Africa

Brigham Young sent missionaries to South Africa as early as 1853. Although the Church existed in that country for 125 years before the 1978 revelation, at no time was the gospel taken directly to the black people. Except for a few isolated individuals, no blacks were members there before 1978.

One of the first blacks to accept the gospel in Africa was William Paul Daniels, who came in contact with the missionaries in 1913. An elder in the Dutch Reformed church, he was impressed with the missionaries and their message. He traveled to Utah, where in 1915 he was baptized. He received a blessing from President Joseph F. Smith that if he remained faithful he would, in this life or the next, receive the priesthood. Hundreds of South African Saints heard his emotional testimony of the power of that blessing. He died in 1936.

His daughter, Alice Okkers of Cape Town, participated in the temple ordinances for her parents. (Her story is found in chapter 20 in this book.)

In the 1940s and 1950s a few people in West Africa began to obtain literature about the Church as they or their friends traveled in America or Europe. Some wrote to the address on the back of the pamphlets requesting more literature and asking that missionaries be sent to Africa to teach them. They received literature but were told: "The time is not yet. You must wait." And so many waited—for many years.

Some Africans in Nigeria and Ghana, on learning about the Church, organized themselves into local churches—a common practice in their cultures. When letters bearing the name of the Church began arriving at Church headquarters in Salt Lake City, the Brethren became concerned. It is estimated that by 1978, twenty congregations totaling some two thousand people in Nigeria alone bore the name "The Church of Jesus Christ of Latter-day Saints."

Glen G. Fisher, president of the mission in South Africa, was appointed to be the first official Church representative to visit these people. He stopped in Nigeria on his way home to Canada in 1960. President Fisher reported to the First Presidency that he found the "Saints" in Africa to be sincere and devout in their convictions about the restored gospel. He recommended sending missionaries to baptize the faithful and establish the Church among them.

The First Presidency called Lamar Williams and others to open a mission in Nigeria. For six years the Church attempted to obtain visas for these missionaries to Nigeria, but when the Nigerian civil war broke out in 1966 the plans were abandoned.

For many weeks before receiving the revelation on 1 June 1978, President Kimball spent much time discussing the issue with his counselors and the Twelve. He also spent many hours in private prayer about this vital matter. In a missionary meeting at an area conference in Johannesburg in October 1978, President Kimball related:

> I prayed with much fervency. I knew that something was before us that was extremely important to many of the children of God. I knew that we could receive the revelations of the Lord only by being worthy and ready for them and ready to accept them and put them into place. Day after day I went alone and with great solemnity and seriousness in the upper rooms of the temple, and there I offered my soul and

offered my efforts to go forward with the program. I wanted to do what he wanted. I talked about it to him and said, "Lord, I want only what is right. We are not making any plans to be spectacularly moving. We want only the thing that thou dost want, and we want it when you want it and not until." (*The Teachings of Spencer W. Kimball*, p. 451.)

Of the circumstances and power of this revelation, Elder Bruce R. McConkie observed: "On this occasion, because of the importuning and the faith, and because the hour and the time had arrived, the Lord in his providences poured out the Holy Ghost upon the First Presidency and the Twelve in a miraculous and marvelous manner, beyond anything that any then present had ever experienced" ("All Are Alike Unto God," Church Educational System Symposium, BYU, 18 August 1978, *Charge to Religious Educators*, 2d ed. [Salt Lake City: The Church of Jesus Christ of Latter-day Saints, 1978], pp. 152–55).

Presidents Spencer W. Kimball and Ezra Taft Benson and eleven other prophets, seers, and revelators were participants in this great event. It is my impression that not only did that revelation come with great power in the temple but that that same power was guiding and blessing a people half a world away—a people who had been so patient and so faithful for so long with so little gospel light. The stories in this book testify eloquently to this power.

Before this revelation the Church did not formally exist among the blacks of Africa. In many respects, this divine directive was the restoration of the gospel for the black people of Africa.

I find many interesting parallels between the restoration of the gospel in the early 1800s and the establishment of the Church in black Africa. Drawing from the oral histories, I would like to suggest some of these parallels.

Parallel 1: Eliases—"To prepare the way"

At the time of the restoration of the gospel, many leaders in other churches had broken away and begun preparing themselves for some kind of message of restoration—Sidney Ridgon, a Reformed Baptist; John Taylor, a Methodist; John Benbow, of the United Brethren in England; and others. To Sidney Rigdon the Lord declared, "Behold thou wast sent forth, even as John, to prepare the way before me . . . and thou knewest it not" (D&C 35:4).

For years there were in Africa unbaptized converts who received divine direction. Many of these had pleaded for direction from Church headquarters; invariably, they shared their new-found knowledge and convictions with those around them—content to nourish themselves with the "crumbs which [fell] from their masters' table" (Matthew 15:27).

One such pioneer was Joseph W. B. Johnson, who organized congregations of "Latter-day Saints" within a radius of seventy miles of his Cape Coast home in Ghana. It is estimated that more than twelve hundred people were prepared for baptism by his efforts. (Brother Johnson relates his story in chapter 1.)

Anthony Obinna, a persistent pioneer in Nigeria, related the following, which occurred in the late 1960s: "One night I was sleeping and a tall man came to me . . . and took me to one of the most beautiful buildings and showed me all the rooms. At the end he showed himself in the crucified form. Then in 1970 I found this book to read. It was the September 1958 *Reader's Digest*. There was an article entitled 'The March of the Mormons' with a picture of the Salt Lake Temple. It was exactly the same building I had seen in my dreams." (Interview by E. Dale LeBaron with Anthony U. Obinna in Aboh Mbaise, Imo State, Nigeria, on 4 June 1988. Also correspondence and other material on file with the author.)

Brother Obinna persistently wrote to Church headquarters seeking Church literature, which he used in teaching his family and neighbors. Little did he know in September 1978, when he wrote a firm letter to the Council of the Twelve, pleading for missionaries, that the revelation had been received and missionaries were on the way. He was the first in Nigeria to be baptized; his wife became the first black Relief Society president in Africa.

Moses Mahlangu, of South Africa, read the Book of Mormon, sought out the missionaries, but was advised (in light of conditions in South Africa) to wait for baptism—which he did for fourteen years. During this time he shared literature with his people and held weekly meetings in his home. Fluent in nine languages, he taught many people. Today, at age 63, he is a groundskeeper at the Johannesburg Temple and the elders quorum president in the Soweto Branch. (See chapter 17.)

Parallel 2: Rapid Church growth

At the commencement of this dispensation the Lord declared that from its humble beginning the Church would "roll forth unto the ends of the earth" (D&C 65:2). By the end of the first decade, the Church's membership had reached 16,865 (*Deseret News 1989-90 Church Almanac* [Salt Lake City: Deseret News, 1989], p. 203).

Following the revelation of June 1978, proselyting began among the blacks in South Africa and Zimbabwe. From South Africa the work spread to the adjacent countries of Ciskei, Transkei, and Swaziland. By the end of 1978 missionary work was under way in Nigeria and Ghana. One year later missionaries were serving in the Mascarene Islands of Mauritius and Reunion. In 1986 the work commenced in Zaire.

By 1988, just one decade after the revelation of 1978, mission presidents estimated more than 17,000 black members of the Church in Africa—a figure strikingly close to the 16,865 membership in 1840, ten years after the organization of the Church in America. Further, the annual growth rate of the Church in Nigeria between the years 1983 and 1987 was 24.6 percent, and in Ghana 37.9 percent. A stake was organized in Nigeria less than ten years after the arrival of the missionaries. Clean, attractive buildings have been rented or built in black communities wherever Church membership is sufficient. In Zaire, a limit has been placed on the number of baptisms per month, in order to allow time to train leaders (the baptism quota is usually filled by the tenth of each month).

Parallel 3: Foundation of leadership

The next four Presidents of this dispensation after Joseph Smith all joined the Church within a month or so of six years after its organization; all the original twelve Apostles were baptized within the first four years. The high-caliber leaders who came into the Church between 1830 and 1840 made possible its survival and growth in spite of the persecutions and hardships they endured.

Africa was similarly blessed with an unusual quality of converts. This is reflected not only in spirituality but also in educational levels. While general literacy in Ghana is 30 percent, and in Nigeria 25 percent (due to widespread poverty and unemployment), 82 percent of the stake and district leadership I interviewed in these countries were college or university graduates. In Ghana, 76 percent of the Relief Society presidents had comparable education; 58 percent in Nigeria. Of the two hundred converts I interviewed in Ghana and Nigeria, the majority (74 percent and 55 percent respectively) had received some college or university education.

Converts among the youth similarly serve with faith, devotion, and spiritual maturity. The children love to sing—and they sing with beauty and feeling. Testimonies of children and adults are strong and inspiring. A nine-year-old in the Aba First Ward fast meeting went to the pulpit and said: "Good morning, brothers and sisters. I am happy to bear my testimony, because I was baptized on conference day. Since I joined The Church of Jesus Christ of Latter-day Saints, God has been guiding me both in the school and at home. Now that I am baptized, I promise to continue obeying God's commandments. I testify that the prophet Ezra Taft Benson is true. I know that Jesus Christ is the Son of God. I say all these things in Jesus' name. Amen." (Tape on file with author.)

Parallel 4: Culture and tradition vs. restoration and revelation

One of the great challenges for Joseph Smith (and Brigham Young also often spoke of it) was to counter the strange beliefs and practices which converts brought with them. Likewise, the first missionaries to Africa "untaught" many traditions—crucifixes and other adornments in the meeting houses, "drumming and dancing," "rolling," and the collection plate.

These practices, somewhat common to many of the churches in Africa, ceased after the people were baptized and the Church was organized among them. When asked if the missionaries made them stop such things, the most frequent response was that once the members received the gift of the Holy Ghost and the priesthood, they did not feel good about doing these things any more.

Parallel 5: "My Spirit upon all flesh, . . . dreams, . . . visions"

Many converts to the Church in this dispensation, including Solomon Chamberlain, Wilford Woodruff, and John Taylor, were prepared for the Restoration through visions and dreams.

Adjei Kwame, a religious young man from Ghana, educated in mechanical engineering in the Soviet Union, kept having dreams of a church building. Traveling through a neighboring town, he saw an LDS chapel and felt attracted to it. In that chapel that day he discovered what and where his dream-building was. (His account is in chapter 13.)

Dr. Emmanuel Kissi, furthering his medical training in England, received at his hospital one day a phone call from his wife, who announced that two young servants of God had called at her house and blessed her, healing her immediately of an illness of several weeks. When Dr. Kissi read of the First Vision, he had a positive but unusual reaction.

The Kissis now operate a clinic, called "Deseret Hospital," on the outskirts of Accra, Ghana. (For Dr. Kissi's account, see chapter 2.)

Parallel 6: Opposition and persecution

Even before missionaries arrived in Africa, the pioneer saints faced great opposition. Many faced the loss of their jobs. Some of their children were publicly ridiculed and even beaten. Joseph Otoo, an early branch president in Ghana, became the target of persecution for belonging to an "American church" (see chapter 4).

They take strength and courage from early Church history and find that these trials have strengthened their faith and resolve. They refer to themselves as "pioneers" in Africa.

Parallel 7: The poor and the meek shall have the gospel

Many of the converts to the Church in this dispensation, especially from foreign lands, were from among the poor and oppressed. They became the foot soldiers of the army of Saints who made the desert blossom as a rose.

It is impressive and inspiring similarly to see many of the meek and poor, even illiterate (they do not speak or write English), in Africa accept the gospel.

Sister Lily Andoh-Kesson grew up in poverty, receiving only part of one year of schooling. As is common in her culture, she did not meet her husband until the day they married. She bore sixteen children, raising thirteen to maturity. She could neither speak nor write English. Carefully considering the Church's teachings, as explained by others, she felt they were true. She was among the first to be baptized by the early missionaries. When the local church meetings changed from her native tongue, Fante, to English, she did not leave the Church, as did some others, but remained true. Twelve of her married children and their families have come into the Church as a result of her influence.

Wilson and Judy Nqunqua, of South Africa, live four hours by car from the nearest branch of the Church, so they seldom have contact with other Church members. As I visited with them through a translator, I was impressed by their faith and humility. On the wall of their small, round, thatched-roof hut hung a framed picture of the First Presidency and the Quorum of the Twelve. A picture of all the Church Presidents hung nearby, and a photograph of the Salt Lake Temple rested on a table.

Parallel 8: The gospel proclaimed by the weak and the simple

The Lord called Joseph Smith, so that "the fulness of my gospel might be proclaimed by the weak and the simple unto the ends of the world, and before kings and rulers" (D&C 1:23). The history of the early Church contains many examples of this.

Many Africans have also fulfilled this prophecy. Julia Mavimbela, a retired school teacher and Relief Society president of the Soweto Branch, South Africa, has discussed the gospel with industrialists and with international political and religious leaders. (See chapter 16.)

Sister Priscilla Sampson-Davis of Cape Coast, Ghana, also a retired school teacher, persuaded her oldest son to give up a lifelong dream and a four-year scholarship to an Anglican theological school in order to be baptized. Twenty months later, he became one of the first full-time missionaries from West Africa. Sister Sampson-Davis was inspired to translate Church hymns into Fante, the language 85 percent of the Ghanaian people speak. Later she translated pamphlets and books, and finally the Book of Mormon itself. At the time of my interview with her, she was at work on the Doctrine and Covenants and the Pearl of Great Price. (See chapter 3.)

I found much evidence of the Lord's blessings resting upon the blacks of Africa, many of whom had been so faithful and so patient for so long. As I participated in this inspiring research project I felt the Lord was saying to these great people: "Be faithful and diligent in keeping the commandments of God, and I will encircle thee in the arms of my love" (D&C 6:20).

It is my conviction that with the marvelous revelation of June 1978 the following declaration of Nephi should be felt in our hearts: "He inviteth them all to come unto him and partake of his goodness; and he denieth none that come unto him, black and white, bond and free, male and female; . . . and *all are alike unto God*" (2 Nephi 26:33, italics added).

These converts of Africa are beginning to have a vision of their important role in the Lord's kingdom. The contribution of the black Saints to the establishment of the kingdom of God in these latter days is perhaps best captured by the story of Brother Jude Inmpey (see chapter 10), a pioneer among the Nigerian saints who was invited to help with record keeping in the mission office. He once attended a social for all mission workers, being the only black present. When invited to express his feelings, he related the following experience.

He had had a dream, whose meaning he had not understood until that evening. He dreamed he was at a social gathering with many people. Someone was playing an organ, but the sound was terrible. People were shouting, "What is wrong with your music?"

Finally someone investigated the problem. "He's only playing the white keys!" he reported.

Then Brother Inmpey observed: "For many, many years the Church has been playing only the white keys, but now we are playing on the white and the black keys, and the music is much, much sweeter."

1

Joseph William Billy Johnson

We Felt the Spirit of the Pioneers

Joseph William Billy Johnson (shown here with Dale LeBaron) is one of the pioneers of the Church in Ghana. In 1964 he first learned about the Church; then, with great faith and perseverance over a fourteen-year period prior to the organization of the Church in his country, he helped prepare the way for hundreds to learn of the gospel. Brother Johnson was born on 17 December 1934 in Lagos, Nigeria, but grew up in Cape Coast, Ghana. His wife, with whom he had four children, left him when he began to give full-time effort to the Church. Brother Johnson was one of the first persons baptized when missionaries arrived in Ghana in 1978. A year later he married Joana Amoah. Brother Johnson's youngest son is likely the only young man in Ghana named Brigham.

One day a minister in my church said to me, "You are going to leave my church very soon. I dreamt of you working with whites, and they said you would join a church from America."

My introduction to the teachings of The Church of Jesus Christ of Latter-day Saints was in February 1964. A friend of mine, Dr. A. Frank Mensah, who was not a member of the Church, gave me the Book of Mormon, the Doctrine and Covenants, and other Church literature. I was a member of the Catholic church, and I believed it to be the only true church. I did not believe there could be any other church on earth that could provide answers to the numerous questions that plagued my mind. My father was a staunch Catholic who played an important role in his church. He always read the Bible and prayed, and I followed in his footsteps—I read the Bible and prayed like he did.

I took the Church literature home and immediately started reading *The Testimony of the Prophet Joseph Smith*. I read other pamphlets, and then I started the Book of Mormon. It took me a month of continuous reading to go through this material.

As I read the Book of Mormon I became convinced that it was really the word of God, and sometimes while reading I would burst into tears. I felt the Spirit as I read. I felt that the book had an inspired message, especially the testimony of the Prophet Joseph Smith. I was really spiritual at this time, and I used to fast and pray. When I read the Book of Mormon I asked the Lord to open my mind to know more about the scriptures and doctrines of the Church.

One morning, at about five o'clock, I got up and prepared for the day's work. When I knelt to pray, I felt transmitted away. I saw the heavens open, and for the first time I saw angels singing praises to God and blowing trumpets. In the course of this experience I heard my name called three times, "Johnson, Johnson, Johnson." And then, "If you will take up my work as I will command you, I will bless you and bless your land." I had never heard such a voice before in my life. I actually heard a voice from heaven mentioning my name thrice and saying I should carry this message to my friends. Trembling and in tears, I replied, "Lord, with thy help I will do whatever you will command me."

From that day onward I was constrained by that Spirit to go from street to street and house to house with Dr. Mensah, who also believed in the Church's teachings. I delivered the message which I had read in the Book of Mormon. I did exactly as the Lord commanded me, and immediately persecutions started. People began criticizing us because they had never heard about the Book of Mormon. We were ridiculed and heckled by mobs, who refused to believe in the Book of Mormon and the Prophet Joseph Smith. They knew only the Bible and would not accept any other scripture. Other churches in Ghana took notice of us and started calling us names. They branded our group as an anti-Christ organization. Anti-Mormon literature said that the white Mormons didn't like the blacks. A Ghana newspaper had pictures of our prophets and filthy statements about them. Persecution became bitter—so bitter that we nearly gave up from the very onset. But through much prayer and fasting, and by the guidance of the Holy Spirit, we waxed strong in the Spirit and continued propagating the gospel without flinching. On Wednesdays, Fridays, and Sundays, we met in the mornings and evenings to study and pray. We avoided the culture tradition of adoring the shrines in town. Our faith grew stronger, and the Lord revealed great things to us—many of the members of our group saw wonderful revelations.

I recall one occasion when we were busy preaching at the Accra Post Office Square, and a group of people who professed to be a religious body suddenly broke up the meeting by distributing anti-Mormon literature. They thought to discourage us, but we were undaunted. We persisted, and won the hearts of forty people that day. They became members of our group.

I had a revelation to gather the believers at one place and teach them the doctrine of Christ. I informed Dr. Mensah of the revelation, and on the sixth of April 1964, I gathered the converts in an Anglican school near my house, discussed the Book of Mormon and the Bible, and prayed with them. The Spirit of God manifested itself to us. We formally organized the group as a church, in line with the Church in Salt Lake City, Utah. We named our church after our mother church, The Church of Jesus Christ of Latter-day Saints.

I wrote to America, asking the authorities to send missionaries to us. At this time President David O. McKay was the prophet of the Church. He wrote back saying, "Johnson, we are with you, but it is not yet time for us to come. So keep on studying the scriptures and wait patiently until we shall be sent to Africa." We received several encouraging letters from the prophet, urging us to study the gospel and help our people until, in the Lord's own due time, missionaries from America would be sent to us.

After working very hard, we were able to establish the Brigham Young Educational Institute, which was a primary school, in Accra. Due to financial difficulties, the school was closed. We waited for the missionaries for some time, but they did not come. Dr. Mensah fell away, leaving me alone.

I resigned from my job in 1969 so that I could take up preaching for the Church. My boss visited me and inquired why I had resigned from my job. He asked me if I was crazy or if I wanted more money—he was prepared to give me more money. But I resigned and I preached on my own, from house to house, spreading the work of God. I continued full-time preaching until 1979.

There was a time when I was very persecuted. People were insulting me and hooting at me. People were asking me why I changed religions, why I joined a church that only believed in Joseph Smith. They said we worshiped Joseph Smith. I had had revelations, but I was still losing my strength in the Lord because the criticism was so great. One night, I went to our chapel to sleep. I prayed, and in tears I asked God to fortify me and strengthen me because things were too hard. Then I slept, and in the night the Lord spoke to me in a wonderful dream. In the dream I saw the Salt Lake Temple coming from on high. That was the first time I had seen the Salt Lake Temple. It was full of light, and it descended to earth. The temple was hollow, so I could see the inside of it. It came to where I was and rested on the ground. Then I heard a voice saying, "Johnson, don't lose faith in my church. This is my true church upon the earth today, whether you believe it or not. I say unto you, this is my true church." I said I would testify of the Church and of all that the Lord had spoken to me.

When I left my work to preach full-time for the Church, my wife left me. She said I made a wrong decision in resigning, and she divorced me. One day when I was sad and weeping because of my wife, I had a dream about my brother, who died in 1969. He was my only brother. He asked me, "Brother, why have you been weeping all night? What is wrong with you?" I said, "My wife has left me." He said, "Don't worry, the Lord will give you another wife, and you have chosen the right thing. You have chosen the right church, and your church is the only true church on earth. It is the church in the place where I am, and I am now investigating it." I was surprised. I had never known that the Church extended to another world. He said, "If you don't believe me, I will sing a hymn from my church in order to show you." He sang "Come, Come, Ye Saints," even though he was a Methodist when he died and had not known this church. Then he said, "Don't leave this church, my brother, don't leave the Church! Please see that I am baptized." I didn't know anything about baptism for the dead. I now know that my brother has received the gospel already, and he's only waiting for me to have him baptized. It was my brother who enlightened me about baptism for the dead. And the Lord did give me another wife.

Later, I also saw my uncle in a dream. He was a staunch Methodist. He said that since his death, he hadn't found a good place to stay and that he was wandering about. He said that he needed me to have him baptized. My aunt also appeared to me and said that I should have her baptized. I am very fortunate that most of my relatives have appeared to me in dreams, asking me to have them baptized. I feel that there are many who are waiting for this work to be done and that it is very urgent.

Once I was reading the prophet Brigham Young's words about the spirit world, when suddenly I felt entranced and saw numerous dead people, several of them calling me by name and referring to me as their great-great-grandson. They mentioned names to me and said that I should tell the names to my mother. They told me about how we depart from this earth, and they said that I should see that they were baptized.

Another time, when I was in Cape Coast in front of a Methodist chapel, I saw a vast number of people who had passed from this world. They were well dressed and had fair complexions, but they were Africans. They said, "Reverend Johnson, do you know you have a work to do for us? Our great-grandsons and great-granddaughters will be in your church soon. See that we are baptized." They said that they had been taught wrongly and needed to be baptized. Because of these revelations concerning baptism for the dead, I am very convinced that this doctrine is really true, true! At times I weep when I talk about it because I see thousands of people behind the veil who are expecting baptism.

When I was about forty, I went to see my father. He was blind at that time. My father was a staunch Catholic, and I tried to introduce him to the Church. He told me to stay away from the Mormons; he didn't want to hear about them. I asked, "Why do you condemn my church? Is my church not good?" He said, "I don't care. I am Catholic." Being his son, I kept quiet for some time, and then he said, "Are you annoyed?" I said, "I am not annoyed. When you speak I should not speak. You are my father, so I should not provoke you." That night we slept. About two o'clock in the morning my father got up and said, "Come, tell me about your church. I've seen you in a dream tonight, and you were taken into heaven wearing a white cloak." He said that in his dream he went into the sky to the place where our Heavenly Father lives. He saw a great number of people dressed in white. There were people visiting around a table, and I asked him to join them. He joined them, and they told him about the Mormons. He said, "Your church is in heaven. I believe what you told me last night. Your church is the only true church on earth, and I heard this when I went to heaven." He started listening to me when I talked about the Church, and he never complained about the Church again. He was searching, but he was old and blind, and he couldn't read about the Church. He was a religious man; he just chose the wrong church.

One week after my father died, he revealed himself to my wife. He had been blind on earth, but he was no longer a blind man—he could see. My wife saw him well dressed, wearing a tie, reading a paper. She said he looked so young. I feel that my father will accept the gospel and become a new man of Christ. I know if I do the work for him in the temple, he will accept it.

My mother was a Methodist, but as soon as I took up the work of the Church, she joined me. My mother is a baptized member, and she has played an important role in the Church. She doesn't hold a position in the Church, but she is a staunch Relief Society member.

In 1977, two priests and one lady, leaders of one of the churches in America, came from the United States to persuade me to change my church and join them. They brought cosmetics and many things, which they distributed to persuade my members to listen to them. They offered to train me to be a minister in their church and to give me a full-time salaried position. They also offered to spend ten thousand dollars on equipment for my church and to give me a free ticket to America. I would have loved to see America. They nearly convinced me, but I was afraid, because I knew the Lord had asked me to stay in his church. So after they proposed all these things to me, I went to my room and prayed. I wept and asked, "Lord, what should I do? I have waited for so long, and the missionaries have not come. Is this not a blessing you want to give me? Should I accept it?" Then the Lord spoke to me and said, "Johnson, don't ever confuse yourself or your members. Stay fast in the Church, and very soon your brothers will come and assist you. Don't move an inch." I doubted a little whether I had really heard the voice, so I said, "Lord, if it is thy voice, show me a sign that you have spoken to me this night." As soon as I came out of my room after praying, one of the priests said, "Johnson, I am not here to change your church. I can't do it. The Lord has spoken to me and has said not to tempt you, for you are sincere about your church, and I shouldn't try to change the name of it. I am sorry. Despite this, though, we shall be friends." We did become friends, and he brought me literature, weird things, that I just put somewhere, and I stuck to my Book of Mormon and other Church books.

I remember another visitor, a white evangelist, who came and performed great miracles. He tried to convince me to affiliate with his group, and he offered me cash gains, but I said no. I wasn't rich; I was in poverty. I kept on refusing the offers from other sects. I felt in my heart that if I changed, the Lord would punish me. I decided to wait for the missionaries to come.

When some members in my group found that I was not yielding to the other churches, they became angry with me, and five of them rushed to my house. They thought that if I gave in to these sects they would have money, and they wanted me to change my mind. I didn't know what to do, so I decided to show them more love and explain the gospel to them. I sat and talked with them, and I embraced them one by one. The last man I embraced wept bitterly. He went down the corridor weeping and then started shouting for help, because suddenly he became crippled and couldn't stand. He confessed that he had arranged for all of them to come on me with force and beat me if I wouldn't agree.

That night, the Lord rewarded me with a blessing, a revelation in the form of a dream. In the dream I was lifted up in the sky until I saw past two levels, to a third level. The first level had a low glory, and I could see that it was a telestial glory. Then the second was the terrestrial, which was a bit better than the telestial. The third was so glorious that I would love to live there forever. A choir of angels, people cloaked in white, were rejoicing, and I was in the very midst of them. I was shown a beautiful mansion, a beautiful city—I can't describe it. I don't think there is a city like that on this earth. I realized that this was a promise to me that, if I live well and keep the commandments, I will be there one day.

It took longer for the missionaries to come than it did for the pioneers to cross the plains. We felt the spirit of the pioneers. In our church meetings I would read and tell about the pioneers, as if I had been with them. From the faces of my members, I could tell that they wanted to hear more about the pioneers. They would say, "Bring a message from the pioneers." We gained our strength from the pioneers. We were inspired by their works. When I would tell of their trials my people would weep, especially when we sang, "Come, Come, Ye Saints." We would also sing "Come, O Thou King of Kings," and when we sang "We've waited long for thee," tears fell from our eyes. We had trials, but we felt close to the Church. Even though the whites were not with us, sometimes we felt they were.

The Book of Mormon is a powerful book, and I got nearer to God when I read it. Anytime I stopped reading or teaching the Book of Mormon, I would get weaker and weaker in spirit. And anytime I taught more about the Book of Mormon, we would be strengthened.

The Book of Mormon worked miracles. In a conference, before a large crowd of people, I was testifying of the Book of Mormon when I felt in my heart that only a few were receiving the message. I felt that almost all were rejecting the message, so I prayed in my heart, saying, "Lord, please open the eyes of these people to see and to know that what I am telling them is true." Suddenly I felt in my heart that the Lord was going to use me right then. I saw in the crowd an old man who was sick, and I said, "Brother, please come." He came, and I held his hand and told him about the Book of Mormon. Then I called elders and told them to lay their hands upon his head and see what the Lord would do. I put the Book of Mormon on his head and prayed for him. He was completely healed. We asked him to bear testimony, which he did in the presence of the people. He started weeping and said he didn't know he was going to meet Christ that day, but that Christ really revealed himself to him. He said he was just walking about when he felt he should come and stand in the crowd, but he never knew that the Lord wanted to heal him.

Once, my old cousin Alice was so sick that we took her to the Cape Coast chapel for the elders to lay hands on her head, but she died. There was a nurse in the church building who tested her pulse and said she was dead. We prayed and then laid the Book of Mormon on her, and in the presence of the elders she got up. She is alive today.

God did these things so that people would listen and read the Book of Mormon, and many people believed and did read it. He showed them signs so they would turn their ears. They said they had never come across such a powerful book, and they started buying the books from me. Many times people who were blind and mad were healed. There was a blind madman, an elder in the Church today, who got his sight. We have a sister who died once, but is now a member of the Church. There was a lady who suffered from cancer and was going to have her breast cut off, but we laid the Book of Mormon on her breast and prayed, and when she went back to the surgeon the cancer was gone. This lady is also in the Church today. The Lord turned the minds of the people to the Book of Mormon, and we would give them a copy and tell them to read it, and they started paying attention to it.

I wanted to be a shining example like the prophets. In my room are pictures of all the prophets of the Church. I wrote to Salt Lake, and they sent me the pictures, so I put them on my wall. One night after I had fasted for three days, I prayed to the Lord, saying, "Lord, reveal your prophets to me tonight, and let them speak to me." I will now tell you why I named my child after Brigham Young. That night in my dream, the prophet Brigham Young spoke to me and said, "Johnson, we are with you, and soon missionaries will come and assist you. I am Brigham Young, who succeeded the Prophet Joseph Smith." In the morning, I was so happy I said I would name my child after this great man of God, which later I did. In my dream I also saw the Prophet Joseph Smith. He said, "Johnson, soon, very soon, missionaries will come. Prophet McKay is thinking of you, and very soon you will have missionaries. Just keep studying the scriptures; we are with you." Then he brought me two tape recorders, one black and one white, and he joined the two tape recorders together, and they became one. He said that very soon I and my brothers in America would become one.

When I had my next revelation about the Prophet Joseph Smith, I was lying flat in a building full of light. Gazing down from a window, he said, "Johnson, pack up and come to where I am." I was inspired by this. The reason why I had these revelations is that we had many challenges, and anytime the Lord realized that we were losing faith, he showed us something to revive our faith in the Church.

We began to have revelations about the coming of the white missionaries. People in the Church would come and tell me they had seen the whites teaching us. One night in a dream I saw whites entering our chapel. They were not walking, but they came from the heavens. They said, "We are your brothers, and we have come to baptize you." They were in beautiful garments, and as soon as they came in our midst I saw several blacks who came from many other churches to join the Church. After this dream, I told the members that I had seen a revelation about the coming of our brethren from America.

One night I tuned our radio to the BBC at twelve midnight. I don't know why I tuned to the BBC that night—it had been several years since I had listened to the BBC—but I did, and I heard the message of President Kimball's prophecy concerning the priesthood, that all worthy males in all of the world could receive the priesthood. I burst into tears of joy, because I knew the priesthood would come to Africa, and if we did the right things, we would all receive the priesthood.

I heard the message in June, and in August the missionaries came to Ghana. The very same day that they came, I had another revelation after I read the Prophet Joseph Smith's testimony about the organization of the Church. I read about the Spirit falling upon the six, and I felt as if I were with that six. I felt the presence of the six leaders who had met together, and then I saw white people coming to me in a dream. I felt that the gospel was being restored and that I was a part of it. Then I saw that the whites had come, and we were together entering into a mighty temple, which was full of light. I saw people that I knew.

We were so happy to receive the missionaries. When the missionaries sat face-to-face with us, many members remembered the revelations they had had, and some of them bore their testimonies in tears. I was one of those who bore my testimony in tears, because I realized that the Lord had fulfilled his promise which had been revealed to us, and all came to pass. Nothing they taught us seemed strange—they simply confirmed what we had heard. We were already familiar with almost all the teachings. When they felt that we were ready, they baptized all of us. We had about six hundred baptisms. I had organized ten branches by the time they came, but only five branches were found faithful, and not all the members stayed. When the missionaries started explaining the Church to the members, some couldn't comply with the Lord's will and with the doctrines of the Church. We had nearly nine hundred members, but about one third of them left.

There was one sister that the members loved and called Mother, because she was like a mother to all of us. She took care of the members, and she lived the commandments. After she had been baptized, she felt that she should have the priesthood. She requested this and was told it was only given to the men. I was surprised that she didn't stand faithful—her trouble was that she wanted to receive the priesthood, which we realized was against the law of the Lord. I don't think even the Lord's mother received the priesthood.

When the missionaries came they started us on the right footing. We started growing and realizing new things about the Church. Because I was alone in the early days before the missionaries came, and there was nobody to direct me, I just directed the Church as I knew how. We had collections to keep the Church going. But once we studied more about the Church, we stopped the collections. Some churches in Ghana have shouts; they sing in praise of God, and they dance. The Methodists turned to clapping and dancing just to win membership. The Catholics were also doing it just to get members. Sometimes they dance in an odd way, but we danced reverently, since I taught the members not to dance like they would in a dancing hall. To keep the Church going, since I didn't want them to leave, I allowed this for a time. Then I said, "No more dancing and no more clapping, since our brothers in America don't do it." I asked them if they would accept that, and they said they would. At times some wanted to clap a little, but we stopped it for the most part, except when we had games and socials.

Some who joined the Church after the missionaries came have accused me of starting the Church the wrong way. They have forgotten that I was alone, without any missionaries, that I was doing it on my own while waiting for the missionaries to come. Instead of appreciating what I have done, they kick against the early practices of dancing and clapping.

From the time the missionaries came, I felt a big weight lifted from me. With more priesthood now, the burden of caring for so many people has lessened greatly, and I feel freer than before. Most members are testifying of the Church and gaining more experience, and that makes me happy, because they are bearing the same testimony which I bore to them years ago, and they are confirming what I told them was right. I feel happy about that.

Today in the Church, some people want help before they do anything. There have been a lot of backsliders in the Church, and many are inactive. They depend upon the leaders, and they ask us before they do anything, and then they want to be assisted in doing it. I used to walk fifty miles on foot and wasn't bothered about it—I felt more strengthened by it. Whenever I walked I reflected on the early missionaries, and it seemed as if I was following in the footsteps of the pioneers. Anytime I walked a long distance in order to preach, I ended up with a lot of strength.

I love working as a missionary more than anything. I love to bring souls to God—this is what I am most interested in. Anytime I visit a baptism, I shake and have tears of joy because I see more people coming into the Church. I have a growing love for missionary work, more than for any other area.

I am still doing missionary work, but not as I was doing before. Each day, my target was to convince somebody about the Church and win them as an investigator. If I didn't speak to a soul in a day, I didn't feel happy. And before the month's end I felt I should get at least thirty people baptized. If I did forty-five or fifty baptisms a month, then I felt more satisfied. When I stopped doing missionary work I felt I was offending God. I felt guilty, as if I was neglecting something precious in my life. The more I do missionary work the happier I become.

I was recently telling my wife that I would like to work for a few more years and then go back to full-time missionary work, this time together as a missionary couple. The work should go on until we have covered the whole of Ghana. Like Alma, I feel that, oh, if only I were an angel and could go forth with the trump of God, with a voice to shake the earth and cry repentance to all people. During all my life, this is all that I have wanted to do.

The Church of Jesus Christ of Latter-day Saints is restored on the earth today, and it is the only true church on earth; it is the Lord's own church. Every living human being should be a member of it and live its teachings so that he may return back to his Heavenly Father. It is the only true church. I have a testimony that it is true, despite every persecution and trial. We are here on earth to pass through many trials, but we will be able to endure these things; they are for our own perfection.

2

Emmanuel Abu Kissi

I Have Found the Fulness

Dr. Emmanuel Abu Kissi, a medical doctor, and his wife, a nurse, operate a clinic outside of Accra, Ghana, named Deseret Hospital. Born in Abomosu, Ghana, on 24 December 1938, he was one of twelve children. He married Benedicta Elizabeth Bamfo on 10 June 1970, and they are the parents of seven children. Dr. Kissi graduated from medical school in Ghana and pursued advanced medical studies in England. The missionaries came to his home in Manchester, England, and introduced the gospel to Sister Kissi. Dr. and Sister Kissi were baptized on 8 February 1979. Dr. Kissi has served as a branch president, a district president, and a counselor in the Ghana Accra Mission presidency.

I will be fifty years old this December [1988]. I was born in the little village of Abomosu in the eastern region of Ghana. I was brought up there, went to school there for six years, then after two years elsewhere, I went to Cape Coast to high school for seven years. Then I qualified to go to the University of Ghana in Legon as a medical student. I qualified as a medical doctor, then went to Kumasi to do my first medical assignment. That's where I met my wife and we married.

In 1974 I came back to Accra to do further studies in medicine, this time in surgery.

In August of 1976 I got a scholarship to go to London to finish up my surgical training and came out of Guy's Hospital as a surgical specialist.

I practiced there for a while, then in 1979 came back to Ghana to take up an appointment as a lecturer in surgery.

In 1982 I realized that this job wasn't sustaining my wife, my family, and myself; it was necessary to go into private practice, which I thought would be more lucrative. Of course it has been better financially, and living has been better, though I miss the joys of teaching.

I have realized that practice has not been as lucrative as I thought it would be. Other practices are apparently more successful because doctors are willing to terminate pregnancies. I do not do such things. They are not legal.

My wife and I have six children, and an adopted one. In Ghana, when a woman dies in a family, her immediate younger sister is responsible for taking up the reins of the administration of the deceased sister. All the sister's children become her children. So when my wife's elder sister died, my wife automatically became the successor of her sister. We took one of the four children and have legally adopted him, and we have cared for the others also.

I grew up as a little-village boy. My father had a large farm, and we were many children—twelve of us, though the eleventh one died. We went to school in Abomosu but on the weekends went to the farm, where there was plenty of food, plenty of meat. We yearned for every Friday evening to come so we could rush to the farm. My father was a very successful farmer. We took back with us enough headloads of food for the week, returning on Sunday in time to go to the Presbyterian church.

When I was about nine or ten years old, in 1948, my mother's mother, who was living alone and was half blind, needed support. My younger sister, number six in the family, was asked to live with the old lady and help her do things. She went but couldn't cope. Then my senior [older] brother, directly before me, went. He also couldn't do it. There was no hope for anybody to live with my grandmother, so I volunteered, and I lived with her. This I did until I had to go to school outside of town.

As her blindness became more severe, I always walked close to her, holding her hand. Sometimes she held a stick, and I held onto the other end. Because of this, everyone used to call me "the old lady's walking stick."

I lived with my grandmother for three or four years, until I left home for school in 1953.

This experience had much influence on me. It was one of the reasons I went into medicine. I felt moved that people who are medically unfit, who are unable to do things for themselves, need someone to care for them. I realized then that medicine was one of the best ways that one would be able to help mankind.

In those days, there were occult practices in our town. Being Christians, our family didn't have much knowledge of what actually happened in the occult. I knew there was drumming and dancing, festivals and other occasions, but we were made to be uninterested. My grandmother once went because she wanted to know why she was blind, why she had this misfortune. In Ghana nothing happens without cause. So there is a lot of witchcraft.

My family was very close-knit. As a family, we thought we were special, and we loved to be in the family. We worked hard. We had everything we needed. When we went to the farm, my father would give us a contract—an idea he got from working with the white people. We each would be given a portion of the farm to clear for the day's work, so we all would weed and clear the land. At the end of the day, we would harvest what we needed and go back home.

Once in a while my father and mother would flare up a bit at each other, but generally theirs was a cordial marriage relationship. I knew of families very close by us in which the parents fought, and it was miserable. We children were happy we didn't have that experience.

My father was a senior presbyter in the Presbyterian church, a figurehead, almost as long as my memory goes back. Even when he lived on his farm, every Sunday he would come back home and go to church to perform his duties. He would conduct the meetings that were necessary and finish the day, before going back to the farm in the evenings. There was a very strong religious influence in our home.

My father doesn't mind my involvement in another religion. When we preach Christ, he is well convinced that we are doing it effectively, so he has no objection. We have tried to get him baptized, and sometimes he agrees and wants to; then later on he says he is old and has been in his church all this time and cannot see much reason to change. He is old and weak, and I suppose we will have to leave him alone.

I remember very well my first day of high school, 21 January 1955, a Friday. I had made up my mind, from my experience with my grandmother, that medicine would give me a chance to serve in the way I thought I should. I realized that day that if you take a certain branch, that is the direction you will go. I decided the way I wanted to go.

I came out of medical school when I was about thirty years old, and thought it was about time to marry. While still in medical school, I didn't have the financial means to do so. Now I had my education, and the next thing was to find a companion in life.

My wife was one of the nurses who worked on the ward in the hospital in Kumasi where I started working as one of a first batch of newly qualified medical doctors from Ghana. She was tallish. I told her senior on the ward that I liked Benedicta and would like to go out with her. The senior said by all means to go out with her, so that's how we got started.

I invited her to my home one evening, to a program the medical association was having. When she came, I was rushing to leave, so I asked her to have anything she liked at the house—to take the key, and I would come back and collect it. She says that impressed her very much—that I had trusted my whole house in her hands. She thought I would be generous in life. So we got on, and soon after got married.

We were married in a nondenominational church, by a Methodist minister, I think. We also satisfied the Ghanaian marriage traditions, being sanctioned by the elders on both sides of the family.

Over the years, I have been very involved in the community, as well as in medicine and the Church. Whenever I attend a meeting for an election, I am invited to run for an office. Sometimes I deliberately refuse to attend meetings, because I don't have time to be an officer. At the present time I am a member of the area council. Accra is divided into twelve council areas, in an effort to decentralize the administration. But basically I don't want to be very much involved in politics. I have been on many committees and councils.

As district president of the Church, I have meetings on Saturday, as well as an area council meeting sometimes. In my Church position, there are some things that only I can do, so the area council people understand if I cannot attend their meetings. I have done more than my share of community work.

I was a Presbyterian until I joined the Church. Like any other Presbyterian, I went to church on Sunday, listened to what the preacher said, came back home, and that was the end of it. I had read the Bible several times, from Genesis to Revelation, and that led me to expect something more than the churches were doing. My secondary school was an Anglican school, so I knew a lot about Anglicanism, but I still felt things were empty. I also took the trouble to look into what the Methodists and the Catholics do. Still I felt that the churches were empty, but Christianity wasn't. There must be something more than what the churches were teaching. So I made up my mind that there was something, but I hadn't found it yet.

Just about that time, I read in one of the local daily newspapers a feature article about the Jehovah's Witnesses. They often made foolish statements which didn't sound good, to my knowledge and understanding of the scriptures. So I returned to the Bible to learn anything I could. I did that for a long time, still having the same feelings of emptiness in the churches. I desired to know more and to find a church that would satisfy my idea of what religion should really be like.

About this time, I received a scholarship to study in Britain—the first time I would be leaving Ghana. To me, London was the center of civilization and the world; if there was anything good in the world, it must be there. I told myself that if I went to London and found no good religion, then I would forget about it. It didn't exist.

My first year was academic work, then we went to Macclesfield, eighteen miles from Manchester, where I worked in a hospital.

One day my wife rang me to say that some missionaries had come to the house and talked to her. For a long time she had not been in much of a mood to work, so she stayed home from the hospital, where she usually worked. She said she felt frightened and wanted to remain at the house.

She had been terribly depressed for a long time. I thought this might be the sort of situation in which a woman feels the absence of her children, so I had her visit Ghana and bring the children back with her. But she still was in the same mood. She would send the children to school, then remain in the house and weep.

Now she had phoned me at the hospital to confirm an appointment, because she was ready to return to work.

"You are kidding," I said to her.

"No, I mean it."

"What has come over you?" I asked.

"Well, I am well now."

Here is what she told me:

"Two young men knocked on the door while I was feeling terrible and weeping. I opened the door. They said they were missionaries and they were preaching the word of God. I invited them in and said, 'If you are preaching the word of God, then come in and talk to me.'

"They came in and I said, 'Before you do anything else, let me tell you that I am terribly depressed. There is something heavy on my mind, on my head, and if you will bless me and I feel good, I will start thinking about whether I agree with you or not.'"

The two missionaries conferred with each other, then came and anointed her. My wife said that in the process of the anointing, she felt something like an electric movement in her, from her head to her feet. And when they finished the blessing, she was cured instantly. She was back to her normal health again.

She had an immediate, instant testimony, and that's why she was so excited to ring me and tell me about it. That was the reason why she was now prepared to go back to work.

She also told the missionaries that I was never at home. I worked twenty-four hours every other day, and on the days I wasn't working twenty-four hours, I didn't get back home till around nine o'clock in the evenings. So they booked an appointment with me at the hospital, and that was the first time I saw them. After that, I managed to come home when I wasn't on duty, so we could meet and discuss.

That's how I got to see the missionaries.

I felt soon that this was the time to find the church I was looking for, so I was keen to listen. I was prepared to listen to see if there was anything new.

The missionaries said that their church was the only true church of Christ on the earth today.

"Nonsense," I said. "If you didn't think your church was true, you wouldn't be in it. Everybody thinks their church is true. That's why they belong."

I gave the example of my culture in Ghana, where people are not supposed to point to their father's house with their left hand because that would be defiling. You use only your right hand. So I was not surprised to hear the missionaries say extreme things. I told them not to make superior statements like that.

We went on with the discussions, and the more we discussed, the more I got interested. I would ask questions, they would answer some. I supposed they conferred with their group on some questions, and even met with their mission president. Then they would come to me with an answer.

Sometimes they had difficulty, and they would say, "Well, we think that if you will read this book, you will find the answers there."

I gave them money, and they brought me *Jesus the Christ* and *A Marvelous Work and a Wonder*. They looked all over England for McConkie's *Mormon Doctrine* but never got one.

I continued to study, because there were still a few questions in my mind. I have forgotten those questions now.

We went back and forth, back and forth, and I think the mission president gave clearance that I could write the prophet.

I was in the process of planning to write, and then somehow I got in my mind a clear understanding to those questions. The answers came, and nobody had told me them. I simply knew that the things the missionaries were talking about were true.

One day they came to challenge me to be baptized, still thinking I would not give in. They came in and I said, "Well, we are ready for baptism."

"You don't mean it!"

I said I did mean it.

They said that by the kinds of questions I was asking, I couldn't mean what I had just said.

I explained that I had to ask questions to satisfy myself. I must look before I leap. I didn't want to jump from the frying pan into the fire. All my questions were satisfied, and I was now ready for baptism.

I don't think they were really convinced until I got into the water. Then they knew I was serious.

I was very much impressed by Joseph Smith's first vision. When I read the story and discussed it, I too was wanting a testimony of the fulness of the truth of the gospel. Paul, who had been Saul, had a breathtaking experience, though I suppose that all of us won't have the same experience. We build our testimonies on what other people have found. I would have loved to have an experience like Joseph Smith had, but he was the one who got it, so it must be a good experience, and it must be true.

All that impressed me very much.

In fact, Joseph Smith's story was similar to my situation. He had the same problem that I had with churches. I just put myself in his place and found myself enjoying every bit of his experience. It wasn't difficult for me to understand him.

The missionaries told me about the Book of Mormon and said it was true. They were discussing points from it. I said to them, "Don't tell me *about* the book, give me one to read. If you have read and understood it, I suppose that if I read it, I would understand it too. When I have read it, then we can discuss; but if you talk about it now, I am ignorant."

They brought me a Book of Mormon, I read it completely through, and then I was ready for discussion. Having come out of medical school, without much reading to do in my work, I had plenty of time and desire to read.

I read it and loved it. That is how I was able to first understand. I suppose the Spirit gave me clear understanding.

The idea of a prophet on the earth is good. In Ghana there are many prophets, so the idea of a prophet wasn't new to me. Of course I always wrote these prophets off, not thinking twice about them—not because there shouldn't be a prophet, but I didn't believe these prophets were what they claimed they were.

I was satisfied with the idea that there can be only one prophet on earth at a time. There can't be two captains on a ship, so there should be only one leader at a time.

I didn't think about the policy of blacks and the priesthood until after I came into the Church. The revelation came in June of 1978, and we found the Church in 1979.

The nurses my wife worked with asked her how she, being black, could expect to be a Latter-day Saint, given the teaching of the Church on blacks. My wife came home and talked about that.

When I have problems like that, I go to the scriptures, so I wasn't worried. My rationale was that the Church was good, even if the Lord had decided that the black man was not to hold the priesthood. Now that the Lord has decided that the priesthood should be made available to blacks, what's wrong? By analogy, the white man in South Africa says that South Africa is right in not allowing blacks their rights of ownership. If tomorrow the whites give everybody equal rights, should the blacks refuse? So why should we blacks refuse to accept the Church? I have no problem with the issue.

Sometime in Britain, when I spoke in sacrament meeting, there was an unusually cool breeze, and I knew the Spirit was with me. Every now and then, in prayers and in conferences, when I have to give a speech, I feel very much the presence of the Spirit.

The teachings of the Church have a lot to offer. Before I joined the Church, I had in mind what the Church should be able to provide. Now that I am in the Church, I think everything is unfolding. Everything that happens in the Church is what I expected to happen. One must, as it were, thirst for knowledge and understanding, and there's no end to the thirst.

The Church has grown in Ghana, though I have felt it could have grown faster. Everyone I have talked to about the Church feels sad that they didn't find the Church sooner. You would expect people to rush to join the Church. But there are a lot of detractors—members and leaders of other churches. They will stop at nothing to oppose the Church. They use politics or whatever is available to try to not let the Church stay in this country to operate. There's a saying among us that if you run from the countryside very fast and hard, you will hit the sea, and that will be the end of your running. You can't run beyond the sea. The enemies of the Church have run to the sea—they have gone to the heights of the government, but have not succeeded. We have been able to open our true hearts for the government to know, so the government officials are not fearful of us. Now our opponents use more subtle means here and there.

If they find that Mormon missionaries have been to a house, the next day they are there. In one case in Accra, the missionaries went to a house, and then the next day some preacher living nearby went to the house and said to the family, "Who are those people who came here? Never let them come in again. They are not teaching the true gospel of Jesus Christ. . . ." And so on and so on.

The man of the house said to the minister, "You have been living here for many years, yet *you* never came to me to tell me about Christ. Now you come to my house and say that what these men are telling me is not true. Never come to my house again, because *you* are the one who is not true!"

So people are making frantic, strenuous efforts to make sure the Church doesn't cover the ground that it should. I think that the Church will, in time, experience geometric growth, rapid increase in membership.

In 1979 when I returned to Ghana with my wife, the presence of the Church was already known. A young man and a few other people in the area had been informed about the Church by Joseph William Billy Johnson and others. Special missionaries had come in 1978. We started gradually and learned correct doctrines. Earlier on, people were teaching the wrong things—drumming and dancing, for example, and collecting plenty of money, as the other churches did.

President Johnson, from Cape Coast, had been very influential in getting the Church established there. I believe it was because of him that the Church grew faster in that district. He says that he went to Cape Coast because it was difficult to operate and preach in Accra, there were so many clever enemies and so many people who didn't want to hear. He was well known in Cape Coast, where he comes from, so he was able to get people to listen. President Johnson, more than anybody else, was active on the missionary front.

Our greatest challenge in the Church is the enthusiasm of the members. Everybody is most happy to be in the Church. They like the teachings and want to be able to live fully according to the precepts and commandments. The only problem is that they are financially handicapped. There are a lot of things they want to do which they cannot do. The branches are far apart; some people have to travel significant distances, and some find it difficult to pay for their transport to go to church. If they were able to move about freely, they would be able to participate in all their programs. They are enthusiastic about activity, but they are sometimes unable to get to church.

The young people who have come into the Church are happy. In Ghana, as in many African places, the younger population is more progressive than the older people. Most of the older people have positions in their churches. Some have confessed, "Oh, I've been in this church for so long, and I would lose my associations"—that sort of thing. But by and large, responsible people are responding to the gospel message.

Though the Church could have probably done all right without me, I think my presence has helped somehow. I have had offers to go out of the country, and my desire to do so was very strong. But I have decided to stay and help the Church, and I am happy I have. If I left, the Church, I'm sure, would go on, but its progress might have been delayed an hour or two. I know others have said I have been a major contributor to the Church, and they may be right. But that's not easy to say.

Ghanaian tradition doesn't have much that is contrary to gospel principles. There are traditional religions in Ghana, from before the white man or Christian doctrine came, but these performances are not necessarily our culture. Religion is a way of life, and so the religious performances easily merge with the performances of local people.

For instance, the chief in ancient times didn't have to have priests, but sometimes, because of wars or other things, he had to consult the priests for prayers. From this, the priests got involved in certain functions and added a spiritual connotation. The rulers often mixed local religion with their ruling, but the traditional ruling isn't necessarily against Christian principles. However, if you allow the local religion to creep into the ruling, then you are in trouble.

My conclusion is that you can be a traditional ruler and continue to be a Christian. We have chiefs here who are Christians. They let the people do a lot of things which they, the chiefs, don't believe are necessary. The chiefs and the people come to terms.

I can wear western dress without offending my people. It is a question of color. In mourning times, you should wear either black, red, or pink, so I couldn't have worn my western dress to my mother's funeral. I have since had a black suit sewn.

In our culture the family unit sticks together closely, and the unit extends beyond the nuclear family. Traditionally, all my brothers' children and my own should call all of us "Father." My younger brother's children call me "Senior Father," and the children of my older brother call me "Junior Father." My children are his children. It is the same with my wife. Our children call her "Mother," and her younger sisters "Junior Mother," and her older sisters "Senior Mother."

We believe we should look after our elderly people too. It is sad when this doesn't happen. People go to the old people's home and lose touch with relations. The nurse will do everything for you, but a grandchild will have a little different touch.

The important question in life is life's purpose. We should want to know what the purpose of life is, and then fulfill it to the letter. Then we would achieve our reason for being here. If you don't know the purpose of life, but beat around the bush, your values are wrong. You may achieve wrong values, thinking you have achieved much. But perhaps it is all vain and useless; it doesn't earn you anything. I would like my posterity to seek the truth, to get to know their reason for being on earth. When they find it, they would do well to adhere to it and fulfill their goals.

Going to the temple is, of course, the climax of a Church member's desire for learning; at least it's the highest spiritual experience one could encounter. My wife and I were sealed by Elder David B. Haight in the Salt Lake Temple, then we went to the Jordan River Temple and to other temples. When you go into the temple, you forget that the world exists. You forget, that is, until you come out and say, "Oh, the world is still around after all." The feeling of the temple is different; you are in a different place.

I don't know what I expected the temple to be like. Before I went to the temple in Salt Lake City, I had a dream, which I told to my wife. In the dream I was in a beautiful room.

After we went to the Salt Lake Temple, we had an invitation to go to the Jordan River Temple. When I went into the celestial room there, the atmosphere was exactly what I had seen in the dream. It was an exciting situation, and I related it to the officiating staff.

When Elder Haight came to Ghana in 1981 to dedicate the land to the gospel preaching, we hadn't had rain for a long time. It rained that day for the first time in many months, and we knew a man of God was there. Elder Haight has been watching my footsteps all the time.

I have found the truth. I have found it! I think of the story of the Samaritan woman who met Jesus by the well of Jacob. After talking with him, she was satisfied that Jesus was a great man, so she rushed to the town and made noise, saying, "Come, come, and see the man who told me everything I did in my life. Might this be the Messiah!"

That is my message: I have found the Messiah. I have found the fulness of the true gospel of Jesus Christ. My message is that people should search it out themselves and prove whether this is not that true gospel in its fulness.

The Church is so true, I don't think I have words to convey the message. We should stick to the Church and hold on to everything it brings us.

3

Priscilla Sampson-Davis

An Instrument in His Hands

Priscilla Sampson-Davis was born in Kumasi, Ghana, on 4 May 1927 to a polygamist family of seventeen children. She completed elementary and high school and then graduated from the College of Technology with qualifications to teach school as an arts and crafts specialist. She taught school for forty years. On 30 December 1956 Priscilla married J. E. Sampson-Davis; they have three living children. Sister Sampson-Davis was introduced to the teachings of the Church in 1964 in Holland when missionaries called on her, but she later joined the Church in Ghana. She has served as a Sunday School teacher and in a Relief Society presidency.

When I was fifteen years old, I was an Anglican, and I went to St. Monica's Anglican College to train to be a teacher. I became a sacristan for the church and was assigned to clean the church altar. The sisters liked me because of the way I cleaned the altar, so I was allowed to count the wafers for communion, and I supervised the girls who cleaned the chapel every Saturday.

During this time, I had a dream, or vision, in which I saw our Lord, Jesus Christ, carrying his cross. He called me by my name, and I came near him and stood before him. He was carrying a heavy cross on his shoulder. He was actually dragging it, for I could hear the noise of the end of the wood on the ground. He wore a crown of thorns, and blood and sweat were coming out from the pricks and dripping all over his face and down to his chest. He couldn't even open his eyes because they were heavy with sweat and blood. He was trying to look at me but couldn't open his eyes. He said to me, "Please, it is because of you that I am carrying this cross. It is because I love you." I stood and stared at him, and I was so sorry and sad that he was carrying the cross because of me. He paused for a while and then asked me, "Please, could you give me a handkerchief to wipe my face so that I can see clearly." I said, "I will do that my Lord." Then the vision ended.

With my childlike outlook, I thought the Lord actually wanted a handkerchief. I knew that the priest used small white handkerchiefs, called purificators, to wipe the wine cups at the altar. Because I cleaned the altar, I knew the size of the handkerchiefs. So, when I was given pocket money, I went to the store and bought a yard of white cloth and cut it into twelve pieces and sewed them into handkerchiefs. Then I sewed red crosses at the corners of the handkerchiefs.

By the time I completed the handkerchiefs it was almost Easter. The night before Easter I bought a packet of candles, because Anglicans use candles, and I put the candles and the handkerchiefs into a small basket and covered it with flowers. Around nine o'clock in the evening, when all the students had gone to bed, I crept quietly into the church and placed the basket by the altar and went away.

While I had been preparing the handkerchiefs and delivering them to the altar, I felt very good. I delivered them at night because the Lord says that you should not let your right hand know what your left hand doeth, that we should pray to our Heavenly Father in secret and he will reward us openly. I had to deliver the basket secretly so the Lord would reward me openly.

From then on, when I would count the wafers, I would see the handkerchiefs I had made and would feel happy. I'd think, "Yes, I have given the handkerchiefs to our Lord to wipe his face." Up till now, nobody knows who put the basket on the altar.

Later on, when I grew up, I felt that those handkerchiefs were not what the Lord meant, that he meant something else. I asked a few ministers about my vision. I explained that I saw the Lord and that he asked me to give him a handkerchief. I told them of the handkerchiefs I had made, and that now I wondered if that was really what the Lord wanted; perhaps he wanted something deeper, something spiritual. One of the priests told me that I should have become a nun. By then I had already married, so I felt very sad for not having asked somebody to enlighten me earlier. If I had, I wouldn't have married, but would have joined a convent and become one of the sisters at St. Monica's.

Later, I spoke with another minister, and he told me that I should resign from teaching and do evangelical work, which would represent the handkerchief the Lord asked of me. I was always thirsty, wanting to know what our Lord actually meant.

After completing a three-year specialist course at the College of Technology, I got engaged to John E. Sampson-Davis and subsequently got married on 30 December 1956 in Holy Matrimony. We had grown up together in the same neighborhood at Cape Coast, my hometown.

My father gave me advice about marriage. He had three wives, but he felt that polygamy wasn't a good thing. There wasn't always peace in his home, and at times when the wives were quarreling he would leave the house. A few years before he died, he called me to his bedside and told me that it is not a good thing to marry more than one wife. He said that a man who marries more than one wife is always a liar, because if you have two wives you always give two tales, so you don't tell the truth. He said that you have as many tongues as you have wives, since you have to say a different thing to each in order to pacify them.

After we got married, I started teaching school. My husband started working in Accra, about one hundred miles away, so I lived in the boarding school, and it was only on holidays and weekends that we were together as a family. We lived this way for twenty-six of the first thirty years of our marriage. In Ghana it is not uncommon for the husband to live in one place and the wife in another so that they both can work, when duty calls. It was very difficult, but we never quarreled, for the time we spent together on weekends was so short there was no time to quarrel.

I loved teaching. I think I am a born teacher. I taught for forty years at girls' boarding schools, and I have always enjoyed good relationships with my girls.

My husband and I are now both retired, and we live near my last school. Some time ago, I noticed that some of the non-resident girls of this school were finding it difficult to get transport to school in the mornings and often missed the first and second periods. They also had to walk a long distance in the heat of the sun to get home after classes. I felt for them, so I asked my husband if we could use part of our house as a hostel for those poor girls. My husband agreed to it. I spoke with the girls' parents, and they were very pleased and said it was a great help.

At the moment, sixteen girls are staying with us. I decided to make an extension to my hostel, which is now almost completed. I hope by next year to recruit twelve more girls, to bring the number to twenty-eight. What makes me happy is that all the girls call me "Mummy," and they call my husband "Daddy." They have taken us as their parents. Though none of them are Latter-day Saints, we have family home evening with them every Monday night. They ask me in the afternoon, "Mummy, are we going to have family home evening tonight?" This contact with the gospel is molding their lives. I feel at peace.

My first contact with The Church of Jesus Christ of Latter-day Saints was in Holland. In 1963 John and I went to Holland, where John worked for the Phillips Corporation. One day I was alone in the house, when I heard the doorbell ring. I ran downstairs and opened the door, and to my surprise I saw two young, well-dressed gentlemen standing at the door. They told me they had good news to share with me, and they asked if I would allow them to come in. I said, "Why not? I am a Christian. Please do come in." They came in and started talking to me about Joseph Smith and the gold plates. It sounded strange to me because I had never heard of it. On the following Saturday they came and met my husband and the landlady, and they started talking to us about the restoration of the gospel. The landlady and her husband didn't like the discussions and started asking unnecessary questions. At that time everything sounded strange to me because I didn't understand it properly. The missionaries gave me a copy of the Book of Mormon. When they came back again the landlady was not friendly at all towards them, so they didn't come anymore—we were just tenants, so we couldn't say much. If the missionaries had come back, I think I would have gotten baptized then.

When I came back to Ghana I met Brother Johnson, who had the Book of Mormon and other Church literature. Even though he was not a member of the Church, he started holding meetings on his own in Ghana. In a conversation I had with him, he mentioned The Church of Jesus Christ of Latter-day Saints. I said, "Ah! I have heard about that church, in Holland." I said I would come to his church meetings.

When I started attending Brother Johnson's meetings, the LDS missionaries hadn't come to Ghana yet, so we were worshipping like the spiritual churches: after reading and preaching from the Bible, the collection plate would be passed, and we would sing hymns, using cymbals, drums, violins, an organ, and other instruments. Sometimes during the sermon, people would dance and sing. After Brother Johnson taught me from the scriptures, I started appreciating the teachings of the Book of Mormon and got to know that it was true. The Holy Spirit made me know it was true.

It was in 1978 that missionaries of the Church first came to Ghana. I was among the first to be baptized, along with all my living children. I tried to get my husband to join, but he wouldn't listen. This made me feel very sad, because I knew the importance of family unity. Anytime I talked to my husband about the Church, he just brushed it off. At times there was contention, so I stopped mentioning it, because it wasn't getting us anywhere. Contention was something I hadn't experienced in my married life, so I decided to take my problem to the Lord. I decided to fast for three days and pray to our Heavenly Father. I prayed and fasted. The second night, when I was saying my last prayer before going to bed, I heard a voice behind me saying, "Your husband will join the Saints." I turned around suddenly to see if somebody was standing behind me in my room, but I couldn't find anybody. I realized at once that it was the Lord who spoke to me. I prayed again and thanked our Heavenly Father for answering my prayer.

My husband started studying the gospel secretly without letting me know. I don't know why he studied it secretly — maybe because he felt proud. Sometimes, while he was looking at the book *Gospel Principles* he would see that I or one of the children was coming, and he would put it away. I told the children to be quiet and to watch what Daddy was doing, but we showed no signs that we saw him reading that book.

One Sunday at sacrament meeting, the names of people that were going to be baptized were being announced. To my surprise my husband's name was mentioned. It was a great joy to the family. Just before my son left for his mission in the United States, my husband was baptized by the mission president.

About two years after my baptism, I had a vision. It was in the morning after sacrament meeting, when I was at home relaxing. I wasn't asleep. I saw that I was at a sacrament meeting, and somebody in white apparel came and stood in front of the stand and called me. I came forward and stood by him, and then he asked me to turn around and look at the faces of the people, to see if they were all enjoying the service. I looked, and I said I couldn't see any difference in their faces. Then the man in white asked me to look carefully. I saw that some of those in the congregation had bent down their heads. The man asked me why those people were not joining in the singing. I told him that they couldn't read English, and so they couldn't sing, so they bent down their heads. He asked me if I wouldn't like to help my sisters and brothers who were illiterate or couldn't read English, so that they too could join in singing praises to our Heavenly Father. Though I could speak Fante, I couldn't write it well. But I didn't say no; I said that I would try, that I would do my best. Then the vision passed away.

Immediately I got up and took a paper and pencil and started translating the song "Redeemer of Israel" into Fante. I was surprised that I could do the first verse completely. I felt very good. This feeling inspired and encouraged me to work around the clock. At times I would do the translations until one o'clock in the morning, go to bed, and then get up at four o'clock and continue until six. I never felt tired.

Just a few months later, I was reading the *Ensign* when I came across an article about the Book of Mormon being translated into another language. I was inspired, and I heard the Spirit saying to me, "Couldn't you do that too?" I said, "Lord, I will do it." Straight away I went into my room and got paper and a pencil, took a copy of the Book of Mormon, and started translating. I discussed the translation with the mission president, and he asked me to continue. I asked him not to tell anybody what I was doing, so we could keep it a secret. I didn't want people to know, because they would start praising me or thanking me, and then I would lose my reward in heaven.

I felt good as I translated the Book of Mormon. I knew the Lord wanted me to do it, because at times, when I would use a certain word or a phrase, suddenly, as if somebody was standing behind me correcting me, I would hear, "No, use this word," or "No, not that word." I always have an eraser with me, because the Spirit is always teaching me. If I make a mistake the Spirit just whispers to me.

When I wanted to translate the name "The Church of Jesus Christ of Latter-day Saints" into Fante, it was very difficult, because the phrase "Latter-day Saint" has many translations in Fante. I wanted to use the best word for the Lord's work. At first I used the word *nkyirmba*, which means "modern." A few days later, I was just sweeping my room when I heard a voice saying, "No, don't use *nkyirmba*, use *ekyirmba*. It is appropriate." The voice told me that *nkyirmba* means "modern," but *ekyirmba* means "people who are coming." All along, the Holy Spirit has been guiding me, and this makes me feel that the Holy Spirit is a comforter and also a teacher.

The Book of Mormon is done. I received a beautifully bound copy of the translation, with President Ezra Taft Benson's signature on the front page. After translating the hymns and the Book of Mormon, I translated *The Testimony of the Prophet Joseph Smith* and other missionary pamphlets. Then I translated *Gospel Principles* and *Book of Mormon Stories*. I am now doing the Doctrine and Covenants and the Pearl of Great Price. I want to finish all the standard works.

The translations have helped members of the Church. I know one sister who is illiterate, an elderly person around seventy or so. At times she says that when she comes to church she just sits there and feels like going to sleep because she can't understand a word —everyone speaks English and she doesn't understand. She says, "Why should I spend money on transport and come to church just to sit, and see people opening their mouths, and not understand what they are saying?" It is language that keeps a lot of people away. It says in the scriptures that in the last days people will hear the gospel in their mother tongues. This is what the Lord wanted me to do, and it is by his grace that I do it.

I now know for sure that by translating I am giving the Lord the handkerchief that he asked me to give him to wipe from his face the sweat and blood dripping from the pricks along his head. The work I do in translating these things gives my brothers and sisters who can't understand English the opportunity to see and read the true gospel for themselves. I see a relationship between giving a handkerchief to Jesus so he could see and translating so that the people of Ghana can see. He has said, "Inasmuch as ye have done it unto one of the least of these my brethren, ye have done it unto me" (Matthew 25:40). I don't need any thanks or praise from anybody; all praise and thanks should go to our Heavenly Father. I am just an instrument in his hands. May his name be blessed and praised.

4

Joseph Kwamena Otoo

I Was Persecuted for My Faith

Joseph Kwamena Otoo is the son of a Fetish priest who had six wives. In the short time that he has been a member of the Church, he has experienced a lifetime of trial and persecution. He was born in Mpintsin, Ghana, on 9 September 1954. After elementary and high school, he completed a higher accounting course from the Takoradi Polytechnic College. In May 1978 he married Joyce Mensah. They are the parents of five children. Brother Otoo was introduced to the gospel by his mother and was baptized on 17 May 1982. Soon after his baptism he was called as a branch president.

I was born on 9 September 1954 in Mpintsin to parents of royal descent. My mother, Akosua Esson, was a queen mother—her ancestors were all chiefs, so her sons were to become kings. My father, Kwamena Dontoo, was the leader of warriors and was also a Fetish priest, which is a witch doctor. His sons were to become chiefs.

My father was known to have a lot of magic. He was a craftsman in the juju, which is the magic in Ghana that heals people. He was the mouthpiece, or the spokesman, for our gods. We had a lot of gods, especially in our area. When my father poured libation or prayed, he mentioned thirty-seven gods, but I'm not sure just how many there were. My father could predict things. For instance, assuming something was stolen and no one knew who took it, if you came to my father he would invoke a spirit to point to the person who took it. He was also captain of the warriors in our area. He had a juice which he used to withstand bullets and other things. He would lead the warriors to battle with other tribes. He was also a physician. On Fridays sick people would gather around him to be healed, and at times they would even stay in his house. When they were healed, they would pay him, and that made my father rich.

People who traveled over one hundred miles to see my father would be charged a higher price, since there was not a witch doctor where they lived. For instance, I remember a group that traveled 160 miles to see my father. A woman and a man had borrowed expensive jewels for their wedding, but the jewels were stolen. No one knew who had taken them, but a woman was accused. My father consulted the oracles. He made certain oracles in a pot and had the accused woman carry the pot on her head. When she carried the pot, a spirit possessed her. She behaved abnormally and irrationally; she shouted and was in a frenzy and even looked aggressive—her eyes became red. At first she could not speak, but my father put a certain leaf in her mouth and then she spoke. The spirit said it wanted compensation, so my father shook the hand of the possessed woman and agreed to pay a compensation to the spirit, if it would find the jewels. The spirit required African food and perfume, so my father cut bread and put it in a pot. Then he took some cloth and some beads, dressed a stick of wood which had been cut in the form of a woman, and offered it to the spirit, to replace the human woman it had possessed. He leaned this wooden form against a tree, along with the food, and he poured libation. The accused woman ran about one hundred yards to a certain tree. Under the tree were some large leaves, and she put her hands beneath them and brought the jewels out, one by one. I was there when this happened. She wasn't from Mpintsin—so she didn't know where anything was—yet she ran and retrieved the jewels. According to my father, the spirit wanted to shame her, so they took the jewels, knowing she would be blamed for the theft. My father was paid.

My father had six wives, who fed him well, so in the village he was considered a rich man. My father was an old man, about seventy-one, when I was born, but he was tall and strong. According to our tradition, the gods continued to make him younger because of the juju he possessed. He lived for about 108 years. The blessings of the gods continued to make him younger and stronger —he never even lost his teeth.

I was the twenty-first son of my father. My mother was his last wife, and I was the youngest of all the children. But I was the one most loved by both my father and my mother. My father wanted me to replace him as captain of the warriors. My father always said I would be the only one to take his place.

So when I was young, at a tender age, I was taught to be a chief, because of the virtue of my birth—I am a royalist of Mpintsin. I was taught all the practices of royal activities, and I planned to be a chief in the future. I grew up in a Fetish environment, where they played the drums and invoked the spirits. I was being trained to follow my father.

The Fetish rites were in the hands of those who were ordained —you didn't have authority until you were appointed. It was not my father's intention to make me a Fetish priest, but rather to make me a warrior leader. He wanted me to be protected, brave, and able to fight. My father told me if anyone beat me and I cried, he would whip me. He inspired me to be aggressive to people. At home he trained me to do bad things to people, but he assured me that if I got into trouble, the spirits and the juju would support me, so I shouldn't worry.

When I was very young—I think I was eleven or twelve—my father delivered me to his warrior group, and they taught me to fight. I had to travel with them to learn what they did. We would walk on foot. I knew how to shoot a gun, and they would train me to fight with my hands and with knives. We were assured that while fighting with another tribe, we shouldn't fear at all, because nobody could do anything to us. My father proved this during the annual festival for his gods, when he hung a garment and shot at it, but the bullet didn't penetrate it—it never went through the garment. We did not use the automatic rifle, just our local guns.

I was looking forward to the day when I would be fortified by taking the juju and becoming immune and protected from the harmful effects of warfare. I would lead people to war with guns, as well as knives and spears. I was looking forward to this, and naturally my father guided me.

However, civilization started to come to our area, and then we discovered that to wound somebody was a sin, and would warrant being prosecuted before the court. Our world changed very fast. The idea of being a captain of the warriors became outdated and no longer necessary. At a certain time, my father decided to make the best of me, and he told me he was not going to allow me to learn the juju, but instead he would send me to school. My father wanted me to learn the white man's way of life, because he said that very soon our traditions would end. Of all my brothers, I was the only son to go to school. The others helped my father in his witch doctoring. Now most of them are illiterate.

I was taken to school, and I did my best. I was always ahead of the class. After my elementary schooling, my father decided that I should continue in the secondary school. While I was in secondary school, my father died, and when he died all his dominion came to an end. All the captains under him separated and scattered, and our house was no longer a fortified area.

My mother loved my father, but was unhappy because of the other wives. The other wives were against her. They would say, "I am the eldest," and when they had to share anything, my mother would get it last. My mother gained nothing when my father died, because the older wives took all his properties—she was the youngest, and there were six of them.

Things then changed very fast, and I could see that to hold to our native ways would mean living in the dark ages. I completed the secondary school with very good grades, but afterwards I had to work because my mother didn't have enough money to send me to the university. She asked me to work, and I gratefully agreed. I looked after my mother, but none of my other brothers did, so she really liked me and was very happy. My mother praised God that my father allowed me to go to school, so that I could earn and provide for her.

I intended to marry a certain girl. When I went to tell my mother about my plans, she told me she had another girl in mind for me. Traditionally, if you belong to a prominent family, parents choose marriages, so I was fortunate that my mother made my choice. If you marry outside the choice, you don't get much respect. I agreed to do what my mother wanted, but I had to leave the girl I had promised to marry. I went to her and explained that my mother wanted me to marry another person. I ended up having to pay her some money, then we ended the relationship. I willingly paid her, since I didn't want to make her unhappy. Then I married the girl that my mother had chosen. She is my wife even now.

My mother was a good woman, a very calm person and a woman of God. She did not attend any church, since my father wouldn't allow it, but I could see my mother believed in God. My father trained four of his wives to be Fetish priestesses, and when the spirits came, they possessed these four wives. However, my mother was never a Fetish priestess, and she wouldn't prescribe cures for the diseased, as did the other wives. When my father died she started searching for a church.

After the death of my father, my mother came in contact with The Church of Jesus Christ of Latter-day Saints. One day she told me she had discovered a certain church. Later she became a member of the Church, and she told me it was directed by white men. She urged me to visit them, but I refused. She told me she wanted me to be a member, but I told her I was not prepared to join any church. Still she insisted, but I just refused.

One day, however, I saw the wisdom in obeying my mother. On Sunday, 23 December 1980, I took my mother to church, where there was dancing and praying. (I was not really convinced about that church.) And then later, on that same day, my mother took me to her new church, and while I was there I saw a certain white man who was a missionary, and by his side was a black man, President Johnson, who my mother said was a leader of the Church, in Ghana. I was given a Book of Mormon.

I hadn't believed in going to church, but when I was given this book I was changed psychologically. I never expected to be a member of the Church, but the Book of Mormon changed me immediately. As soon as I read it, I had joy in my heart. Although I had not read very far in the book, and didn't really know anything about it, I started telling people about it. When I met my friends, something would tell me to tell them about the Church. I was more or less an investigator from that time on.

I received the books *Gospel Principles* and *A Marvelous Work and a Wonder*. I read a lot, and then I went and met with the priest of my former church. I told him, "Chief, I have read a certain book, called *Gospel Principles*, of The Church of Jesus Christ of Latter-day Saints. I am surprised that while here in our church the Holy Ghost is bestowed upon somebody by dancing and shouting, this book says no one can obtain the Holy Ghost without having hands laid upon him by someone who holds the higher priesthood." This priest disagreed with me and told me I was preaching false doctrine.

I was still investigating in 1981, when I was made an instructor in the Sufokrum branch—although I had not yet been baptized. I took my appointment very seriously, and I started working very hard in preaching the gospel. Since most of the members were illiterate, I could be a tool in teaching them because of my education. I saw that I had the qualities of a missionary and that I could bring people to God. So I never rested on my horse—I did all that I could.

When the missionaries from America said that dancing and drumming were not for sacrament meeting, some members felt that the missionaries were coming to take away their liberty. They disagreed and there were problems. One man told us he wanted to break away and form his own church, because he was not going to allow any white man to dictate to him. This man had more than one wife, and he believed that in order to have the Holy Ghost a person had to be possessed; he also believed in collections, and dancing and drumming. He eventually did break away.

Some people didn't like me, because I agreed that we shouldn't play the drums and I refused to dance and shout—I would remain seated. I would sit down and wait. This brought trouble, but I stood on my guns. I never hid my feelings. I was open and frank about not having plural marriages and so on. I knew the Church would not collapse. I felt the Church was strong. And moreover, almost all those people who wanted to leave were illiterate. Many left the Church, but I and others felt we must do what was written in the Book of Mormon and *Gospel Principles*. Since we were new to the Church, we just took our direction from these books.

In December of 1981 there was a coup in Ghana, and a new government came into power. The white missionaries left, so there were no more missionaries in all of Ghana. I was longing to be baptized, but none of the black leaders had the authority to baptize. My mother and I started holding Church meetings in Mpintsin, although we had not been baptized at that time. We did a lot of proselyting, and eventually Heavenly Father started to set his eyes on us. Soon people started joining us.

While preaching, on the Sunday morning of 16 May 1982, a certain white missionary, Elder Kenneth Willit, came and told us that he had come to baptize me, my mother, my sister, and her two children. We agreed, and on the next day, almost a year after I had become involved in the Church, we went to a beach and were baptized. I was made a priest in the Aaronic Priesthood. I felt different after I was baptized. My morals rose high, and I worked a lot and brought people to the Church. I felt strengthened, and I had peace, despite all that was going on. I had peace with myself.

Once we were baptized, the Church had more or less been established at Mpintsin, but there were a lot of problems. The government newly in power was saying that anything from America would destroy Ghana's peace. They said that The Church of Jesus Christ of Latter-day Saints was no exception, and because it came from America, it had all the ingredients for creating confusion in Ghana. As a result of this thinking, anybody found to be a member of the Church was to be prosecuted. We had a lot of persecution, but we didn't care. We continued going to church. The Church had flourished at Mpintsin—many people joined, and there was happiness every Sunday.

On 19 June 1983, a year after I was baptized, there was an attempt made on the life of the head of state. About three days after this attempt, while I was going to work, I was stopped by a carload of soldiers and policemen. They asked me if I knew anything about The Church of Jesus Christ of Latter-day Saints. I said yes, and then I was told to get in their car. They took me to the air force base, where they shaved my head and put me in prison. They threatened to shoot me, and they asked me many questions. I didn't know what I had done, and they never allowed me to defend myself. At that time, I was the branch president in Mpintsin, and they thought that I, being a leader of the most flourishing branch in Ghana, had some knowledge about the assassination attempt. They said I belonged to a church which distributed lies about the government. They asked why I opted to join an American church. I pointed out other churches in Ghana that came from America and said that my church was causing no more problems than any other church. However, they became annoyed and said that I was difficult and was not trying to help them in their investigation. They threatened to shoot me if I didn't tell them all I knew, but I didn't know what to say. I never had any good food there, so I became very lean.

My mother was not worried. Anytime she came to visit me in prison, she said that I had not done anything wrong, that I was being persecuted for my faith, and therefore I shouldn't worry, that they couldn't do anything to me. My mother was a courageous woman, a strong woman, and she made me become more comfortable.

After a week in prison, the commanding officer visited me and asked me questions. He told me about a report from another town, where some officers collected some Church books and said the books were antirevolutionary. I told him that I was prepared to give them Church books, and then he said that if I didn't produce the books I would be taken to Accra.

I was taken to Mpintsin bare chested—they had taken all my shirts. When people saw me bare chested, they stared at me. The officers took me to my house and searched every part of it. I found a book, which I gave them, that concerned the duties and blessings of the priesthood. They were expecting it to be a poisonous book, a book to persuade people not to support the government, but when the officer read a bit of it, he said it was only a church book.

Later, I was released from prison. Before I left, an officer threatened that they would get me at any time, if they were not satisfied with my comments. They threatened that if even one or two people were seen going to our church at Mpintsin, they would be locked up, or even shot down. During that time, shooting by the soldiers was a common thing, done indiscriminately. In fact, people wondered why they had not just killed me. Finally I returned home.

I was released on a Friday night, and two days later, that Sunday, I was at church, shaved head and all. I told the few members there that the Church should go on. I had faith. When I prayed, something told me that the Church was true, so I continued going to church, and people continued to come.

In 1983 I was arrested more than sixteen times, all in only one year, until I nearly lost my life. I was much disturbed by this. In the mornings, while I was getting ready to go to work, a policeman would come, arrest me, and take me away. I would be gone for two days or more. At that time I was working in a cocoa-processing factory. My managers all had faith in me—they felt my case was genuine, so when I had to miss work due to being detained, I still received my pay. My boss thought that I was only being persecuted.

The enemies of the Church knew that if I was killed the Church would not grow, since I was the Church's only strong advocate. That is why I was their target. Most members renounced their faith —about ninety percent of them ran away because they didn't want to be molested by the soldiers. When I was being persecuted, nobody would walk with me; nobody would come to my house or do anything with me, since they might be arrested or killed. Many withdrew and would not attend church. One of my counselors, who used to be a strong member of the Church, fled.

On 3 November 1983, around half past five in the evening, I had just returned from work when a carload of armed men pulled up. They told me that I had been advised on several occasions to leave my church, and since I was not obeying, they were going to take me away. I was ready to go with them, when one of them suggested inspecting my church house, which at that time was in a government school. So I was escorted by these men to the church. There were about six of them, and they were all armed. Many people saw us, but during that time, nobody interfered when you were arrested, because they would also be arrested. So people just looked at me helplessly.

While I was with these men, who were both in front of me and in back of me, something told me to get away, but it was almost an impossible task, because they were watching me. Although I was escorted by them, I just quietly walked away. I never ran, but just walked, and they didn't see me. When I had reached a certain point, I took to my heels, and by the time they saw me I was nearly fifty yards away.

Later, I heard they had combed the whole town but never could find me. That night, I slept at the cemetery, up in a tree. There are wide trees in the cemetery, and its very scary to go there. At about four o'clock the next morning, I left and went to another town.

I didn't understand why this persecution should happen to me. I decided to go to the commanding officer before whom I had been brought more than sixteen times, and ask him why they were doing this to me. I had a little money in my pocket, so I was able to go. Early in the morning, I knocked on the door of the commanding officer. Since by then he knew my name, he said, "Father Otoo, what are you doing here so early in the morning?" I nearly wept. I sat down and said, "Sir, I have been disturbed. I am persecuted because of attending my church. I know you have some headquarters at Accra, and I would like to go there, because every day people want to kill me. Today, I ran away from some men who wanted to kill me, and now I don't know what to do." The man sat there for a few minutes, then said, "I have discovered you are a gentle man, and these people are just trying to disturb you. Yesterday afternoon I received an order to arrest you, but I refused." He then asked me if I could identify those who had just tried to arrest me, and I said yes.

After he changed into his uniform, we left in his car, in search of those men who had tried to kidnap me. This commanding officer thought it wise to threaten the regional secretary, telling him that if, from that time onward, anything happened to me, he would be killed. He said this while I was there, and then he told the district secretary to take a piece of paper and write a statement that said that nothing would happen to me. He told them I was not trying to overthrow the government, that I was a simple man who lived in a village, who didn't own a house, and who didn't have any money, and that he couldn't imagine such a person could overthrow the government. The district secretary agreed with him and said he would see that those men would leave me alone. Then the commanding officer calmly drove me to my house.

Later, it was reported that I had paid one hundred thousand cedis to the commanding officer to exonerate me, but I never had a penny. I am just a simple worker, and I could never have one hundred thousand cedis. If I did I would have been a rich man, which I am not.

Less than a week later, this militant group was dissolved. They had formed in the wake of the revolution and tried to make scapegoats out of many innocent people like me. The head of state had all of the group's members arrested. So those people who had persecuted me, and who had wanted to kill me, are now dead.

After this happened we were free, and I saw the working of God, that Heavenly Father is on our side. During that time of persecution, when I didn't understand why such bad things should happen to me and to the Mpintsin branch, I read what happened to Joseph Smith. One evening, in late November 1983, when I started to see that the persecutions were dying out, I wrote a poem:

> Total capture of a soul, body and mind combined,
> Straighten them for the work of the Savior Jesus' grace.
> Spring out from the people, let our firstlings bear
> Fruits, so precious, so different from other men.
> Let's see visions of joy pouring on as rain
> On the heads of us who are your recaptured seeds.
> Protect us, guard us from evil's lying prey,
> Satan in confusion terrified, stricken, departs.

We had nearly eighty-five members before the revolution. During the revolution it decreased to ten. Soon after everything was put in order, we started to grow, and we produced a lot of missionaries. In Mpintsin, we produce more full-time missionaries than any other branch in Ghana. Right now we have nearly sixteen missionaries, and we have many returned missionaries in our branch. Our branch has flourished, and now Mpintsin is nearly a Mormon village.

Our branch soon spread to other places and became quite large, so in 1985 President Cunningham found it wise to divide our Mpintsin branch into several branches. On 23 February 1986 I was released as a branch president and called to the district council. Later, I was made second counselor to the district president. On 29 November 1987 I was made branch president once again.

Three of my brothers are in the Church, so none of them are prepared to be a chief, as my father was. The chief's duties entail many Fetish activities, but it is not the same as it used to be—not at all. There have been many cultural changes in Ghana. I got out of the whole thing. In my family, I am the only one with a higher education, so I might have been the best choice for chief. But since I have been in the Church, I have not even been invited to attend the Fetish councils. My other brothers, who are not in the church, are the ones likely to be throned. The senior brother likely will be the chief. I hope that he is picked.

5

David William Eka

Growing with the Church

David William Eka became the first African to preside over a stake in black Africa, when the Aba Nigeria Stake was organized on 15 May 1988. President Eka was born at a Protestant mission in Etinan, Nigeria, on 20 May 1945. The eldest of eight children, he faced many challenges and responsibilities. He experienced the horror of civil war and witnessed God's hand in preserving his life. President Eka was one of the early pioneers to accept the gospel in Nigeria, and he has served in many areas of leadership. He witnessed the growth of the Church to the creation of the first black-African stake.

My father was a servant to the early missionaries of the Qua Iboe church, an offshoot of the Scottish Missionary Society. He decided one day, when he was about twelve years of age, to go to the mission to look for a job. When he went there, what little clothing he had on was in tatters. He was given a job, and he lived in the mission until he was about thirty years old. While staying there, he was asked to get married and choose a profession. At a certain age, no one could live in the mission home without a wife. He had to come back home to look for a girl to marry. My mother was just returning from Accra, Ghana, where she had been working as a housemaid. She had no reservation in marrying my father. My father later became a carpenter.

I was born on 20 May 1945 to a humble village home in Etinan. I was the first of eight children and was kind of a pampered child. I grew up in a quiet environment in the village and did all the things that the village children did. I went fishing and farming, and helped my parents. When I was four I was hospitalized for almost one year. At five years of age, I went to primary school. We went to school a distance of about three miles from home, trekking the distance barefoot under the hot sun; the sands were really very hot.

In a typical African setting, much responsibility is placed on the first child. The first child is groomed to replace the father at death. He must inherit what the father had, and then share some with his brothers. The first child is supposed to train and educate the rest of the children. If the first child is not up and doing, then the home cannot make it. I gave my parents support. I was alongside my father in his carpenter's shed. I did all he could do. I did certain jobs when he wasn't there, and that helped train my brothers. They had to follow me, to saw and plane the wood and fix the chairs. My grandfather was a canoe builder, and my father learned the carpentry trade from him. We in turn picked it up from my father. That is how it should go in the traditional African way. The first child is everything. He is the heir to the throne.

During the time my father started contractual business, I used to do market surveys for him, I was thirteen years old then. He introduced me into the business, and I still have that business acumen today. We would travel a day's journey from our village to Aba, to procure materials for the business. My father had no formal education. He couldn't write. I would shop around and buy everything he needed. I would supervise some of the contracts he was awarded. I would be there at the site, supervising the workers and paying them. Out of the very poor and humble beginnings of our village status and with my little effort, my father became an owner of a good house. We were all living in mud houses before, but now we have a block house with a zinc roof. This is a big thing in the village. I, as well as my five brothers, had a good education. My dad is very proud today that in the village, though beginning with almost nothing, we have almost six boys and one girl who have graduated from higher institutions. We are very happy when we go home, because we have something to show for the humble beginning from which we started.

My dad is very dynamic. There was a spiritual awakening in him. He brought us up in the way the missionaries had brought him up. I was an all-round boy in the Qua Iboe church. I participated in the Boy's Brigade, the choir, and the cleaning of the chapel. We served as much as we could. My father was very energetic when it came to church and mission work. We grew up under strict discipline, and if we did wrong we had to pay for it with some strokes of the cane.

When I was young, I was much involved with two churches. We lived very close to the Salvation Army; my mother's people, our next-door neighbors, were of this group. Because of the drums, we children all loved the Salvation Army. We all wanted to play the music. I belonged to the corps cadet. The Salvation Army was exciting because of the testimonies, the drums, and the marching. Since my father was a member of the Qua Iboe church, I was also active there.

Between thirteen and eighteen years of age, my Sundays were very full. About six o'clock in the morning the chapel bells would ring for morning prayers, after which we proceeded to wash in the stream, clean up, and go out in the localities to teach in a nursery program of the Qua Iboe church. A typical setting consisted of an hour devoted to discussion on the subject of the day. At the end of the lesson we went to the different villages and communities. We usually dressed in white shirts and white trousers, which was our Sunday dress. We went out two by two into these areas of the church, to teach and train the younger children. We would tell them Bible stories until the main church service began about ten o'clock. We then came back to the dormitory to have a late breakfast and a rest. About one o'clock we would go out again for the Sunday school, this time to go longer distances and return about six in the evening. We would trek as far as six or eight miles to teach the people. In the evenings, we had prayer meetings in the chapel. We normally had a guest speaker and sang until nine o'clock. On Sundays we were all very busy.

I was in my final year at technical school, in Enugu, when the Nigerian civil war broke out. Behind my school was a rail line that brought casualties from the northern part of the country. I saw men, women, and children. Some were killed, others had legs and hands cut off. This hardened me. I felt sad and said to myself, "Northerners, you cannot do this to us, irrespective of the remote causes of the war." The war was bad. I felt agitated and bitter. I decided that if dying was needed, it was better that everybody should die.

I returned to Aba, but Aba had fallen to the federal troops. I became a refugee. I couldn't speak the Ibo language. I had no money. I proceeded to Umuahia and lodged with others on the verandah of the post office until somebody recognized me and took me to his house. There were many sleeping in this apartment, and some in the corridor. Later I joined the army. I was trained, then sent out to the front. The war toughened me up and made me independent. I lived with the Ibos. I fought beside them. I suffered with them. I could not communicate with them, but I showed them zeal, because I believed that somebody had wronged us.

I felt that the Lord was protecting me. During the war, I stumbled into a house and picked up the book of Psalms. I tucked it into my pocket and went into the warfront with that book. I read it every night and prayed. I gained confidence in God and in myself. I remember one tragic experience. I was with about ten officers from our company, and we'd just deployed our men. We went into the bunker and were playing draughts [checkers]. I heard a still small voice in me that said, "David, move out of the bunker." So I said to the officers, "Gentlemen, why don't we go look at our men in the trench?" They said, "If you want to go you can go. We are playing." No sooner had I left than a bomb was dropped on the bunker and buried all the rest of the officers. I don't always want to remember the war, but it was really an experience. The war made me be a man.

With the assurance that my life was being spared, I knelt down in the bush every night and prayed. I remember in my prayers, I used to say to God, "If you will take me back alive to my people, I will serve you. I will do much more than you ever wanted me to do." I even made some promises that I would train people who had lost their parents during the war, or people who were destitute. I am doing that now, because my wife and I have with us two grown-up orphaned girls that we have sent to school. One is even now in the high school. We sponsor and train her, as part of the promise I made to God. We would say she is our daughter. People don't know, unless we tell them, that she is from another family. We've accepted her as our own. When we came to Port Harcourt, we found another girl wandering on the church premises. Upon investigation we found that she was destitute. We spoke to her relatives and told them that we wanted to take her into our home and train her. We have trained her and supported her through school. In this manner I am helping. Now that I know what fast offerings are all about, I think they are the extension of my earlier promises to God.

I feel that God was preparing me for this day. I want to tell you that I never had a wound in the war, not even a scratch. The only thing I had was malaria fever.

My parents didn't see me for thirty months. They thought I was dead and gone. On 10 January 1970 I walked back home after the war. I went back on Sunday morning, so fewer people would be home, as I didn't want people to see me coming back poor and barefooted. As I walked into our compound, my sister screamed and said, "If you are a ghost, then don't come. If you are a human being, then please come." The noise she made raised the neighborhood, and people started running to see whether it was true that I had come back.

Since my wife's family lived close by, she ran to see this man who was returning from the war. She had attended the same school and the same church as I had. We had everything in common. We understood each other, so when I proposed to her four years after returning from the war, there was no disagreement. She just looked at me and said, "Are you honest?" I said, "Well, I am honest, and I am walking right to your parents and telling them the same thing." I walked to my father-in-law and said, "I want to marry your daughter." He looked at me and said, "David, I know you very well. Are you honest?" I said, "I think so." That is how our engagement started.

Early in 1970 I learned that the Mobil Oil Company was starting production in Eket, so I went in for an interview and was hired as an instrument technician. That was a milestone in my career, changing from electrical engineering to instrumentation. I served offshore with Mobil Oil Company from 1970 to 1976, holding the position of technician foreman in instrumentation. I couldn't advance more, because of my educational background. By then I was just newly married, and I thought about what I could do. My wife and I decided we should go over to England to improve our lot. Our first baby came when we were about to leave. My wife enrolled in a national higher education program in business studies and management. I stayed in Middlesborough for three years, studying instrumentation and control engineering. I had to return to Nigeria and do my fourth year in the National Youth Service, while my wife continued her studies in England. It was after this year that I decided that I would pitch my tent in Nigeria, and that my wife should come back and join me. We had another baby in the United Kingdom, and that was an additional burden.

Prior to this, we knew about The Church of Jesus Christ of Latter-day Saints, because my uncle was a member of the Church, in Wilshire Ward in California. He had written to us and told us about the Church and sent us the Book of Mormon and *Joseph Smith's Testimony*. I didn't read the Book of Mormon that much, but I was thrilled with the Joseph Smith story. "Could this be true? Could God talk to people in these days?" I asked. At the time, we were in Europe. It was interesting that in all the places we lived, we had missionaries visit us. They would always invite us to church, but the distance was the barrier. We couldn't afford the bus fare, so we kept dodging the missionaries. We would meet them on trains, and even after we moved to a new house they came ringing my bell. I said to myself, "The Mormons are never tired."

Each time they came, we told them we'd heard the story before, we knew about the Church, it was true, but we were a bit skeptical about rebaptism. We felt that our local preacher had the authority to baptize us.

By the time I came back to Nigeria in 1979, the Church had sent special representatives Edwin Q. Cannon and Rendell Mabey. They were already in Etinan, running the Church. I was called upon to help them. I went around with them, translating Church materials into local languages in the areas where they were trying to establish the Church. It was then that I really knew what the Church was all about. I remember there was also a time that we had to have some selected portions of the Book of Mormon translated into the Efik language, and I was asked to proofread them. To be able to proofread them and say that the translation was accurate, I had to read completely through all of those Book of Mormon selections. That gave me a chance to know what was in the Book of Mormon. At the end of it, I knew it was all true.

I remember at that time, when I wrote back to my wife, who was still in England, I said, "I don't smoke anymore, and I don't drink. I am a member of The Church of Jesus Christ of Latter-day Saints now, and I've been made an elder." She wrote back, "Do you know what you are in for? Being an elder is not easy." By the time she came back and saw that the little excesses in my life—the drinking, the smoking—were gone, she was thrilled. She quietly started investigating the Church. It is traditional that the wife should follow the husband in whatever faith the husband belongs to. I did not push my wife. I just quietly went about my business. After about a year she realized that I was in a good church, with no more smoking, drinking, or outings, and I was always at home reading my books. Out of the blue, one day she said, "I want to be baptized." I said, "You're not ready. You haven't passed through the lessons." She said, "You bet I have. I've done it all." I didn't know that she was reading my books when I was away. When I would drive in she would close the books.

After my baptism and after serving in callings, I really knew why I was baptized into the Church. I've had humbling experiences in the Church. I worked side by side with some of the first missionaries here. I have served under all the mission presidents in the

Nigeria Lagos Mission—Brian Espensheid, Sylvester Cooper, Duffy Palmer, and Robert E. Sackley. The experiences I had with these great men is what is helping me in this new calling as stake president.

I have also served in other capacities in the Church. I organized the Church in Port Harcourt in the hectic days when there were just five members. We stayed firm and strong, and we knew that nothing would stop the work. It was just a matter of time before the Church started growing. I was with Lamar Williams when he came to visit people with whom he had corresponded. As a result of that visit we organized the Church in Aba. I always lived by the words spoken by Elder Derek Cuthbert, of the First Quorum of the Seventy, when he came here in 1980. He said, "Nothing will stop this work." I felt very good. That has been my guiding motto: Nothing will stop the Church.

The greatest Church growth has been in the cities, because there we have people who don't have to worry about the little things of life; these people can give to the Church and not ask the Church to give anything back. With this sort of people, we can easily build the Church. But then we must not lose sight of the poor among us. I hope more stakes will come up, and I hope a temple will be here one day. What we need to do is get more dedicated men into the Church. The challenges in the local areas are the challenges of leadership.

The next barrier I see is the language problem. Once you leave the wards in Aba, and you get into the branches or the wards in the villages, you find that you are dealing with natives who want to have everything in their own dialect, which I think the Church should focus on in the future. This is one of the challenges the Church must face. And when we do this, the people will no longer feel that the Church is a white man's church. During testimonies the interpreters create gaps that break the fluency of our inspiration. The people don't pick up all that we are saying. And sometimes when we go in and sit with them, they cannot express all of their feelings to us.

Another area we must address is the welfare program. We must look at projects that can feed the people, provide all the nutrients they will need, provide health teachers, and set standards in eradicating certain communicable diseases, such as malaria. These are the challenges that I would say we are going to face, now that we are organized into a stake.

The first black-African stake of the Church was organized on 15 May 1988 in Aba, Nigeria. I was then serving as the district president. But I am not from the Aba area. I don't speak the language. I am from a different tribe, from the Cross River area. I knew many people did not want a man from another tribe to be called as the stake president in their own tribe. Even though we have drummed into the people the realization that the Church must cross tribal barriers, it is still difficult for people to accommodate this. I knew there were sad feelings against me being the stake president. Before the call, I knelt down in my house and prayed, "God, I don't want to be stake president, but I want you to call somebody who will be able to lead the first stake in Africa, because I feel the whole world is looking at this stake. If mistakes are made in the choice of leaders, it could be the mistake of a lifetime for us."

As I drove to the mission home on Saturday the fourteenth at about ten o'clock, I was met by President Robert Sackley and Elder Neal A. Maxwell. I had met Elder Maxwell before. We exchanged memories of the last visit, and he asked how prepared we were. I told him I had twenty-three able men for interviewing. These twenty-three men and I all filled out forms on which we each recommended three persons for the new presidency. When we went in for the interviews, we were soul-searched regarding our moral standards, our capabilities, and why we had recommended those whom we named. After all had been interviewed, Elder Maxwell called me again. He interviewed me again on my worthiness and asked me whether I could stand in the house of the Lord. I said I could. He said, "Then you have been called to be the stake president."

I cried. I felt the responsibility was too much on me. He asked me to choose my counselors. When I was alone, I knelt down and prayed. I had an experience I had never had before. I felt the Spirit prompting me. I wrote two names on a paper. Elder Maxwell came into the room again and asked, "Have you done your chores?" I said, "Yes, Elder." He said, "Who?" I just showed him my paper. Those were the same names he had written on his paper. He showed it to President Sackley and said, "Isn't the Spirit moving?" I was thrilled that my choices and his were in line. I felt the Lord actually chose the counselors for me that day.

I didn't think I would cry on Sunday when the stake was organized, but when my name was read as the stake president, I could not even bear my testimony. I cried throughout. I told the people that it was not because I was unhappy, but because I was looking at my imperfections. I was crying at my responsibilities. I was crying at what lay ahead, and not at the call.

I always maintained that both my parents would embrace the gospel, because they lived close to the missionaries. They have the feeling of The Church of Jesus Christ of Latter-day Saints. They know that the gospel is true. My mother belongs to the Women's Society of the Qua Iboe church, and she says, "When I die, how many women do you have who will sing around my bedside?" I tell her, "It's not the number of women to sing around your bedside that matters, it's where you will be at the end of death." My father, too, had that feeling, because he was big in his own church. But a time came when he started seeing a big change in me and in my brothers who also joined the Church—how dedicated, how honest, how industrious we all became. I think it is through that dedication that he came into the Church.

I remember when Elder Hancock was in Etinan, when he was building the first chapel there, he used to teach my father the gospel in the evenings. My father was about ready for baptism when the Hancocks left, but no missionaries were very close. Then he had a stroke two years ago. He couldn't move. One of the motor functions in his brain wasn't working anymore. I took him back to Port Harcourt. I cried as I lifted my father up every day to wash him and to put him on the toilet. The experience was one I'll always remember. I had the privilege of caring for a father who has all along cared for me.

During that experience my father saw how much devotion we had to God, in praying that he could move and help himself. I want to leave a testimony here that the Lord did a miracle. We don't know how. One fast Sunday, as we came back from meetings, my son, who had stayed home to care for my father, said, "Daddy, Granddad moved out of his bed and came back." I couldn't believe it, but while my boy was talking to me, my father came walking out of the bedroom. I couldn't believe it. I cried when I saw him walk. "What happened?" He said he didn't know. He felt like he was sleeping, and somebody asked him to get up. He woke up and received a partial healing. He is quite well now and is back home in the village. We taught him about the Church while he was with us. When he went back home, people from his old church came to him and said, "Where were you?" He said, "I don't want to talk to any of you, because none of you visited me for the six months that I was away sick. None of you asked. If my son belongs to a society, as you say, I want to belong to that society." He even told his preacher that he had seen the power of God. He had seen his grandchildren praying for him, something that he couldn't do at that tender age. He felt that our church is true. My father got baptized into the Church, and he is now an elder. We are happy. We are thrilled, and we hope that the day will come that our mother will also follow us into the Church. I am also really looking forward to the day when I will be endowed, and sealed to my wife in a temple of the Lord.

I would say that spiritual progress is like climbing a ladder. You just start at the bottom rung and then climb to the top. A friend of mine said to me, "I've not seen you on Saturdays and Sundays. I come around, and each time I come your children say you are out to the church. What do you get out of the Church?" I told him, "You cannot see what I get out of the Church until I leave this existence. You will see my children, if they follow my footsteps, and my great-grandchildren. We will leave a name, a righteous posterity. That is what I get out of the Church."

I believe that future generations of Nigerians who listen to what we are saying and who consider the beginnings and the difficulties —even though we have not been able to tell in detail what we passed through—will realize that we are climbing the spiritual ladder. About nine years ago, when I visited branches with the missionaries, I never believed that chapels could be built here. But they were built, and we now have improved chapels and stake centers. Things are now happening. We never believed we could be organized into a stake, but here we are. Generations of future Nigerians will come and see temples. The Church will reach out everywhere. Stakes will reach to every corner. They will say, "When did it all start?" I know of people who left this church because, they said, we were too slow. Some said, "We cannot wait any longer, David. We have to join our old church." Some of them are coming back. It is a question of being patient, growing with the Church, listening to the gospel, paying tithing and fast offerings, and lifting the Church into the highest heights. I think people should accept the gospel, start from the bottom of the ladder, and climb up to the top. That is what I would tell them.

6

Faustina Aba Haizel

The Church Has Touched My Life, Polishing My Whole Being

Faustina Aba Haizel experienced trials and abuse as a child and as a young woman. Her experiences brought much pain and deep scars which only the gospel has been able to heal. Only through divine help, along with her courage and faith, has she been able to endure and progress. She was born on 9 September 1957 in Winneba, Ghana. After years of struggle and suffering, she heard of the gospel and joined the Church in 1985 in Lagos, Nigeria. Since then she has served as a Relief Society president. As a dressmaker, she supports herself and her ten-year-old daughter.

While I was a young child, I never saw my real father. He rejected my mother (they were not married), so she struggled on her own until she had me and was later married to another man. When I was age thirteen, my father came to take me, but I did not accept him. I think people advised him to come and take me back to his family and support me, but I did not go. I could not turn my back on the man who *did* take care of me all my life, and whose name I bear.

My mother's own mother died immediately after my mother was born. Since my mother didn't have anybody to support her, she was raised by aunts and uncles. She waited a long time to get married, until I was about six years old.

Because my mother never had a parent, she didn't really know how to be a mother. She was too young to understand how. I grew up doing whatever I wanted. I think that is why I fell a victim to the kinds of situations I did. I know both my parents are good; they just didn't know how to take care of me. I wasn't taught any religion or morals. Also, my father was always moving from one place to another, and sometimes I would be given to somebody—a relative or friend—to stay with for a week, until my parents were settled and would come for me. There is no place in Ghana that I have not lived.

When I was very young, between ages fourteen and fifteen, I went out with my girlfriend. Her brother said he and I should go out. I was tricked, and I got pregnant.

I went back to my family, who were angry with me. I moved from where I had been living into the village, where many people didn't know me. So there was not much humiliation, because my friends were not there. My father would not talk to me for the whole nine months until I had the baby.

When the baby was about three months old, my mother and father said I should go back to school. The child is now part of his father's family, though I go and see him sometimes, and he knows I am his mother.

Within a year, my schoolmate died, and we all came to the village. I went out with a girlfriend again, and we met her friend's brother. We had some drinks, I became intoxicated, and the man took advantage of me. I got pregnant again.

In our village, it is always a source of pride for a girl to go to secondary school, so people who knew I was in school were jealous of me; they wanted that opportunity. So when I failed the second time, my mother especially was very angry with me. She decided I should have my own way and do my own thing.

In the beginning, I had almost no money. I would go out in the morning to the place the fishmongers came and buy small bits of fish I could afford. I would carry the fish on my head and hock it around town. The young girls would laugh at me, because I had had the opportunity to go to school and become a lady and work in an office, and now I was selling fish. But I didn't have any choice but to continue to struggle to fend for myself. At that time, the father of my unborn child had not come to accept the pregnancy. I was between seventeen and eighteen years old.

Finally he came and performed all the customary rites and took me away. I came to my mother to have the baby.

After the baby arrived, the man wouldn't come a second time to see us again, so my mother, being angry, said I should fend for myself again.

I would send my junior [younger] brother to the mother of the father of my first child. She was a baker. My brother would buy bread for me. Early in the morning, about four-thirty, I would wake up. I would first sweep and clean the house. My mother would not allow me to leave my baby with her, so about five o'clock, I would put my baby on my back, carry my bread, and go around selling. I always made sure I got to my friends or regular customers early, so I could be sure of getting enough money for my baby's breakfast.

My mother thought she was punishing me for what I had done, and I think that was wrong. But I don't blame her. She didn't really understand.

All this was very difficult for me to do, because I was ashamed to meet somebody I knew, because of all the opportunities I had lost and the position I was in. But I had no choice.

In my father's house, I was just like a slave. My mother would let me do all the work. "If you don't go to school, you have to be a house girl," she would say. When my father left home, I had to make sure his lunch was ready. My mother didn't allow any of my junior brothers or sisters to help me. So I sold my bread, came back home again and did washing, ran to the market, and ran back to cook.

I also had to pound the *fufu*, a local food we prepare. I pounded the yams in a mortar. You use one hand to turn the yam as it is pounded, and someone else is supposed to help you pound as you turn. I had to do it alone.

Then, one afternoon while I was preparing my father's lunch, I heard a knock on the gate. My husband had come back to apologize and take us back. So we went to live with him.

Unfortunately, while I was carrying my third baby, the second one died. She had a convulsion, and I didn't know what to do. She would suddenly shout, then get very stiff. I tried to calm her down and give her food. I just looked at her while she died. Nobody was at home. When somebody came home, she was already dead.

By now I realized what a mess I had made of my life, and how bad everything was. I was very heavy with my third baby, and I felt empty and sad. The day my second baby died, there was a very heavy rain, which I felt was for my baby. When people were around, I would go off by myself and cry, because they would not let me cry when they were around. My mother would shout, saying that in our culture it is taboo for a pregnant woman to be crying. But I always felt like crying, so I would hide myself and cry my heart out. After I felt all right again, I would come out.

Comfort came only when I had my next baby.

However, I kept on struggling with my husband. When we had decided to marry we hardly knew each other. Neither of us understood what we were in for. I decided not to go back home and let my parents tell me, "I told you so."

Things went from worse to worst. He often didn't come home. He didn't care whether we slept or ate. He lost his business and then tried to do "money doubling," or gambling. Then he lost all his property too. We were always fighting, and sometimes he would beat me for no reason.

One day he hit me under the eye, and it swelled badly. I went to the hospital, and from there I went to report to my grandfather, who had my husband arrested. My husband later signed a bond that he would never touch me again, and he never did. I don't know his whereabouts. I am planning to let my parents and his parents know what has happened and to ask them for a divorce.

All this time I didn't know anything about God. I went to church, but I didn't know anything about kneeling down and praying for help, so I kept struggling on my own.

Then one day I just asked myself, "What is really my mission on this earth? Why am I living? I don't have a job. I don't have many children. I don't have a profession. What am I doing? I don't think I should live." I was very confused.

So I decided to go to church and find out if I had a purpose in being here. I went to the Baptist church, but wasn't satisfied. I went to Assemblies of God. I wasn't satisfied there either. I went to Christ Evangelist. I changed churches every day.

Before the whites came here with Christianity, we were all idol worshippers. When local people saw others turning to Christianity, they decided to find ways to get them back. So they started to build churches and do other things, saying, "This is not witchcraft." So we do have many churches like that in our midst.

Such churches do not say anything about salvation. They don't talk about the law of chastity. Nobody in these churches cares about that. People go to them for healing, or to get a husband, or to get money, or to get a good married life—even though they never get those things. They are told stories, or to do this or that. Maybe for a time your problems are solved, but later you get the same problems back again. So people have little faith in such things as going to the church to pray. That is very common in our society.

Then one day a cousin visited me and said, "I heard that you decided to change your mind and live a godly life and become a Christian."

"Yes," I told him, "but I am not satisfied with what I get from any of the churches."

He told me that he was investigating The Church of Jesus Christ of Latter-day Saints, and I should come to it. He thought I would find answers there.

This was a Saturday, so the following day I went to the address he gave me. In fact, on the way to church, my little girl asked me, "But Mommy, why are we changing churches every day?"

I told her I was looking for the right place. Until I found it, I would keep changing churches.

My first impression of the Church came from the reception the members gave me. It was so warm it made me afraid. I had never felt like that at anytime in my life. As I arrived, the meetings of the morning branch were just over, and people were coming out. They all shook hands with me and smiled. I even thought that maybe they were occult and were trying to deceive me, to take me inside the church and kill me or something.

I had not seen anything like this before in my life. Nobody had ever loved me. Nobody had ever really cared for me. Nobody had ever told me to go such and such a way in life.

I was very impressed by the people and by the first lesson, and I wanted to know more. In fact, I was so impressed that I wanted to finish the lessons within a week, and get baptized.

I also received a copy of the Book of Mormon, but I was afraid of it, because I had heard people say, referring to a verse from the book of Revelation, "Don't add or remove." So every time I took the book to read it, I felt nervous and panicky.

One afternoon I knelt down and prayed, "My Father in Heaven, so many things have happened to me in my life. At this time I want to know the right way to go to live the rest of my life. If this book is true, let me know."

Then the missionaries gave me a triple combination. I opened it to section 138 of the Doctrine and Covenants. It told of the Lord's visit to the spirit world, explaining what the Apostle Peter had briefly said (see 1 Peter 4:6). It explained everything and led me to understand that it was true. So because I knew that section of the Doctrine and Covenants was true, I knew the whole book was true, and the Book of Mormon too. I decided to be baptized into the Church. I was baptized on the twenty-first of December 1985.

After my baptism, I felt good and sure of myself, and close to the Lord. I felt light and whole and clean. Now that I have the gospel, I know my past is forgotten. It is gone and doesn't bother me anymore. I don't feel bad about myself anymore. I am a changed woman. I just want to stay in the gospel.

People would say, "The Americans are deceiving you."

I would reply, "Whatever the Americans do, I don't care. I know the gospel is true, and I know it came through the American continent. So I don't have any ill mind about any American. So far, all Americans I've met have been nice to me. I will do my best in my part of the world."

After I was baptized, worldly problems became secondary to me. I overcame my temper. One day a new wife of my husband came to my house to misbehave. I became very angry. I wanted to give her a good beating, but I didn't. The neighbors came and took her away.

Later, the girl's father came to my house and said, "I am very impressed by you." The girl's mother and sisters had all complained that he should come and take me to the police station, but he knew, from what my husband said, that the fault was his daughter's. My husband had told him, "Maybe your daughter did something to her, because that wife is a changed woman."

That's what the father of the girl told me — that my husband was impressed by my behavior. The father also told me that I should remove that offense from my mind and remain steady with the gospel. He knew that Sarah could tell Abraham to send Hagar away, so why didn't I tell my husband to send that wife away — even though the wife was his daughter. He hadn't known that my husband had been married before. That is what he told me.

The missionaries in the mission home have always helped me forget my sorrows and problems. And I also have a special friend, Sandra Rogers, who has had a great influence in my life. She was living in Lagos to do her doctorate work.

She took an interest in me. She went back to America in February [1988], then returned in June. I was down and very sad. She said she wanted to comfort me, but I wouldn't give her the chance. I never wanted to invite her to my house, because I have always had the impression that whites live in a unique environment, and where I live is not good enough to invite a missionary or white person to. So I never invited anybody.

We were having a lesson in Relief Society that said that we in the gospel are "no more strangers . . . , but fellowcitizens" (Ephesians 2:19). I told Sandra that I had always really wanted to invite her to my place. She said she didn't mind how I lived, so I invited her.

She humbled herself to the extent that she slept on the floor with me. The toilet facilities in my home are poor, but she didn't mind.

She came to my house again and invited me to where she lived. We read the scriptures together, and that was the first time I had had that type of experience.

Even today I receive letters from her telling me how much she cares for me. She told her mother about me, and now her mother is writing to me. They make me feel as if I am very important. They give me the feelings I never had even from my parents, the feelings I have never had from anybody. I told Sandra that she has showed me the life I think Christ wanted his children to have. I will send her my birth certificate and other papers, so that should I happen to die, she can go to the temple and do my temple work for me.

She lowered herself to befriend *me*—somebody who doesn't have any background. I am nothing that she should become my friend.

There are many changes in my life. I have learned to control my temper. Whenever I worry about something, I can open the scriptures or the *Ensign*, and something will talk to me directly, as if it is teaching me step-by-step how to live my life.

I have polished the English language, as I have learned to write letters to friends and family. I have a better sense of humor. I have an altogether different understanding of things now, a different look at things in life, although I still struggle very hard in Nigeria.

My job can't sustain me and my daughter, but I don't care. I go broke to the extent that I don't even have one naira, but I don't care. I know always that the Lord will provide, and he always does, no matter how bad it gets. Sometimes I will not get what I want at that moment, but I think of that as a way of strengthening me to push along and not give up.

I have read a lot about the pioneers, especially Eliza R. Snow. She left a good example for me to follow. She was a strong woman, and I hope I can live a quarter of the life she lived as a Latter-day Saint.

The Church has touched my life, polishing my whole being. Outside and inside, I am being reformed and remolded. People around me, my neighbors, see the difference in me. They see me reading the scriptures, and ask how soon I am going to become a priest. They expect me to return to my old manners tomorrow, but that is what only they think.

Now that I'm in the Church, I have hopes, even though I don't have any money to make those hopes stable. I know the Lord lives, and if I keep on living the principles of the gospel, he will help me in anything I want to do. I have been able to find work as a fashion designer, since the ability to sew is a talent of mine. I have been able to save a little money to buy the equipment I need for my own small business. My plan is to go home to Ghana, get some money, and establish my own small way, to live on my own and take care of my child.

The gospel has done so much in my life. It has taught me to be courageous. It has taught me to be strong. I'm no longer afraid of the world. I know that as long as I keep the principles of the gospel, then I don't have anything to fear.

I have heeded President Spencer W. Kimball's counsel to keep a journal. In my journal I always talk to my grandchildren, although they are not here yet. I know they will be. I've told them that I never had the opportunity of growing up in a Christian home, but I know the gospel now and am doing my best to impart my little knowledge to my child. Whenever we kneel down in the morning to pray, we ask our Heavenly Father to let her serve a full-time mission and help her to look forward always to getting married in the temple. I always pray that she will be humble and obey and do these things. If she does these things, my posterity will be happy.

In my journal I tell my future grandchildren about my experiences on the bad side and the good side; I tell them to keep pressing forward, and not to lose hope. The Church is true, and that is the only way they can have inner peace and joy. So they should do their best to live the gospel.

7

Stephen C. Ejielo

Seek First the Kingdom, Then Retain the Spirit

Stephen C. Ejielo was born into a polygamist family on 25 December 1947 in Warri, Bendel State, Nigeria. After completing his elementary and high schooling, he graduated with a diploma in microwave transmission from the School of Telecommunications in Lagos, Nigeria. He then completed graduate studies in the United States at Harris Satellite Communications in Florida. While in Florida, Brother Ejielo learned about the gospel, and he was baptized in Melbourne, Florida, on 15 May 1983. In June 1986 he married Esther Ihuoma in the London Temple. They were one of the first couples from black Africa to sacrifice and save in order to be married overseas in a house of the Lord. Brother Ejielo has served as a district missionary, as a branch president for six years, and in a district presidency.

I was born in Warri, in Bendel State, the first son in a family of six brothers and sisters. I did my primary school in Warri, then left for Sepala, also in Bendel State, for my secondary school.

I'll always remember the great love my father showed to his children. He always made sure our clothes were sent to the cleaners and that they were ironed for us to put on, especially on Sundays. When we went to church, we were all well dressed. He would also try to see that we went to school and had the books or uniforms we needed. He saw that we paid our school fees on time and that we were driven to the school.

My father was a hard-working man, trekking more than three miles to go to work every day. In the evenings, I would trek up a mile to meet him on his way home and carry his pack, which contained his cobbler tools.

In the evenings, he would sit in his easy chair, and I would sit by him. I enjoyed scratching his back as he told me stories about the past and about how I could live to be good. We learned about the scriptures, and he encouraged us to participate in activities, such as the choir, in our church.

My dad was a polygamist. He lived with his first wife for seventeen years, and they had no issue. Then she told him that she was tired of living alone, and that if he didn't marry another woman, she would leave. So out of love for his first wife, he married another wife, who eventually became my mother. We all lived together in great love. My father's first wife treated us like her own children, and that helped us to live in love.

My father maintained the two wives very well in the home. One wife would cook one week, and the other the next week. We always had things in common. My father ensured that the two wives lived together peacefully. We were always happy.

When the Nigerian civil war started, I joined the army at the very young age of sixteen. I experienced very horrible things during the war, in which I served as a signaler. At times, I narrowly escaped death. These were very frightening experiences, but I learned some great lessons. I learned that if you pray to God, he will answer your prayers. I was in the forefront of the battles, always praying that I would survive the shellings and artillery in the bush. I will always remember the promise I made. One day I promised God that if he would lead me throughout the war, I would live to serve him and keep his commandments.

Our brigades were once cut off in an attack, and we were in a place where we had no communications. Headquarters merely came with helicopters to drop us food. We were told there would be no reinforcements; we should try to save ourselves. But there was no way, because we were surrounded by enemy troops.

In the middle of one night, we were able to open a corridor and break through the defense. One man in front of me shouted out that he was tired of the war. Our commander ordered that he should be bayoneted, or he would betray our position. He was bayoneted and pushed aside—a great horror to me.

When we crossed the corridor, I met a young girl of about twenty who had been trapped. Many civilians had already died. I told her to follow me, but she fainted, so I carried her. My friend, an officer, told me that I shouldn't be carrying a woman while we were under fire. I told him that if it was the will of God, the girl would live, and so I carried her across many obstacles.

We met a major who put his pistol to his throat and killed himself, because he thought there was no hope. We passed him and met two young girls crying and holding a captain. I found out he had taken some poison and was dead.

We never thought we could survive. Still, I carried the girl, and when we came to another village, I told her she could go. She was grateful that I had helped her out.

It was in those circumstances that I kneeled down and asked God if he would help me out of that place. I promised to serve him if I lived.

A few days later, some young men came and told us that the war had ended. We had been fighting for two weeks after it had ended, because we had received no communication. We embraced one another, threw away our arms, removed our army uniforms, put on civilian clothes, and walked away.

Luckily, I was alive. But my father had been killed in 1968 by a rocket in an artillery shelling. So my mother and little brothers and sisters had to start life afresh.

In 1971 I was able to get employment in the Ministry of Communications. I served in Sokoto, in the northern part of Nigeria; then, in 1974 I was transferred to Mena, also in northern Nigeria. In 1977 I left for Lagos for a three-year course in microwave transmission engineering at the School of Telecommunications. After my course, I was posted back to Owerri, in Imo State. Then in 1983 I had the opportunity to go to Melbourne, Florida, for further courses in satellite communication.

It was in Melbourne in the Adolf Hotel, that somebody introduced me to the Church. I went to eat, and found a place in the restaurant where one man was sitting alone. I asked him if I could sit with him. He said yes.

He asked me where I came from. I told him Nigeria. He asked what I was doing in Florida. I explained that I was taking a satellite course. Then he told me that he wanted me to come to his church. I told him I would be happy to, and asked for the address of the church. He explained a few things, and the next day, a Sunday, I got dressed up and took a taxi to the ward meeting place.

I was very happy when I entered. Only two blacks were present, a woman from Uganda and myself. The way the people helped me and treated me made me feel more loved than I had ever felt before. The whole atmosphere was very nice.

After the meetings, two missionaries were assigned to teach me the gospel. I gave them the address of the hotel where I was living, and they booked an appointment.

They came during the week, and I introduced them to my roommate. Both of us started taking the lessons together.

We were both baptized after the lessons. I was baptized on 15 May 1983 and was ordained to the priesthood.

The missionaries were very, very good to me. They took me around, and I always kept in touch with them.

The thing that impressed me most was the Book of Mormon. It had a great impact on me. I read almost half of it in one night.

The day I was called on to give a testimony in the ward, I stood and faced the people. It felt as if I were in the kingdom of God.

When I was told of the Word of Wisdom and the law of chastity, I stopped doing things that these laws said were wrong. I started knowing things I didn't know before, and I started hating things that were wrong that I did before.

After making my wartime pledge to serve God, I was always worried, because I was not able to do the things I felt I should. I was always attending many churches to see if I could find a way I would be able to keep the covenant I had made. I was breaking many commandments, and I felt pains in my body, which worried me a lot. My mother, seeing that I was not well, was very worried about me. When I became a member of the Church, I was very happy, knowing that I was going to be able to keep my promise. I learned that I was created in the image of God, and that it was the will of my good Father that I should live a good life and have the privilege of coming back to him.

When I was baptized, I felt I was on a new path in life. I was very anxious to go home and tell my family about the new church I belonged to. They have not yet joined the Church, but I know they will. They are beginning to see the influence it has had not only on me but also on them. When I use my priesthood to bless my little ones, and they become well, my family believes that there is something in this church. Now that the Church has come to Onitsha, only six miles from my place, we are trying to get my parents to start attending meetings.

I came back to Nigeria, where I began work in the satellite section of the domestic satellite. I found a small unit of the Church in Owerri. After six months, I was made the branch president, serving from 1984 until 1987. I also met my wife here.

During that time, the branch grew and was split into two branches, and I was selected to be the president of the new branch.

In 1987 I was released and made the first counselor to the district president. I am very grateful for the opportunity to serve.

It seems to me that if you want to get a wife who will help you have a good family, you can either convert her or marry a woman who is already in the Church. The day I met my future wife, Esther, she told me that she was being plagued by some evil spirits. If I married her, I would have to live with this condition. She had been taken to many medicine places.

I told her that I would like to marry her, and that she would become well when she accepted the gospel and became a member of the Church. That had happened in certain instances.

We went to a place to collect roots and herbs, which we thought might help to heal her, but when we arrived, we met a man who started telling us stories about how he had gone to Egypt and learned the job of healing he was doing. We saw things in his house that weren't very nice. He had a certain mirror through which he tried to analyze what was wrong with somebody, and he had a bed with a red and white cloth on it. So we stood up and told the man that we were sorry. We had come to get roots and herbs, and our church didn't allow us to use services such as he was offering. We couldn't do that anymore. So we left.

My life has been one of undergoing great trials and successes. One striking part of my life happened in 1986, when my wife and I decided we needed to be sealed in the temple. We were married in April, and on 14 June 1986 we had enough money to travel to the London Temple.

My life is now very different in the way I feel. Whenever I am tempted to do something not good, I always realize that it is not good. That helps me to do the things that are right.

I think the greatest change I've experienced is in my family, because when I read about the gospel, I learned that I must prepare myself to be a good person in order to get a good wife.

I met Esther, my future wife, the day I went to visit her brother; we were trying to have a family home evening. She had some clothes to sell. When I saw her, I told her about the gospel and gave her a tract.

Two months later, she and her brother met me again. I was told by her elder sister that Esther used to have frightful nightmares. I told her sister I would pray, and that if they had faith in God, Esther would be all right. We gave Esther a blessing, and I gave her some books to read and advised her to pray and read the scriptures before she went to bed.

Gradually she became interested in the gospel, and we started to go to teach her. It was some time after she was baptized that we decided to marry.

One day she visited me at the office, and as I was seeing her off, the thought came to me, "Why don't you marry this girl?"

She asked if I would marry her. I said I had just then felt that I should marry her.

She left and came back, saying, "Do you not want us to be friends?"

I looked at her and said, "I want to be friends."

"Then will we be married?" she asked.

"I said, "Yes."

Since then, I've found her to be a really wonderful lady.

We made a decision to be married in the temple because of one of the things I read in the Doctrine and Covenants. The missionaries I met with told me a lot about the temple. So I felt I should go to the temple and have those experiences, and enter into the new and everlasting covenant of marriage.

I also wanted to go to the temple to keep myself pure, because my wife continued to have frightful nightmares after we were married. These were disturbing, but I told her that if we could go to the temple, she would be healed.

We went there, and she is now healed. This strengthened our testimonies. When we entered into that covenant, we really knew that God had helped us to get there.

To save money to get to the temple, we tried for six months to limit our expenses to things we needed, forsaking things like new clothing. Our diet was limited to things that wouldn't waste much money. We saved the maximum we could, and prayed, and some of the missionaries helped us with money. I didn't know we could make it so soon, but the Lord helped us.

When the taxi dropped us off, and we saw the temple, I said to my wife, "Darling, this is the house of the Lord." We went in, were received, had our recommends checked, and then were ushered in. I felt that this building was really the house of God, and I was very happy that I had tried to live worthy to come there, because if I had not, I would have been very unhappy. The Spirit was there.

It is difficult to explain how I felt when we were sealed at the altar. I knew that I was doing something very, very sacred and that I must never go against it. When we came out of the temple, we felt we had achieved the greatest thing in our lives.

Since I have come into the Church, I feel I can do many things to show my love for my father. One of them is to get my genealogy records and be baptized on his behalf. I know that he will be very happy. He looks upon me to do that. I strongly feel that he will accept the gospel because he believes in it and loves it. He always tried to do things that showed us a good example.

I would give my posterity the counsel that the Prophet Joseph Smith gave to Brigham Young when he appeared to him and told him that the Saints should seek the Spirit and retain it.

Also, people should know that the choice in life is not between being famous or being obscure, and not between being well-off or being poor. The choice in life is between good and bad. We have to make the right choices with respect to our challenges. We know that our premortal life was with our Heavenly Father, and we know why we are here in mortality. We have difficult challenges, but the Lord has counseled us to seek first the kingdom of God; then all other things will be added to us. We can know and do the things that are good—read the scriptures, be active in the Church, and live as examples of truth and righteousness. In this way we'll be able to prepare ourselves for eternal life. I know this is true.

So let's seek first the kingdom, then retain the Spirit. The Lord will pour out more blessings than we can receive.

8

Florence N. Chukwurah

I Had Peace....
A Spiritual Satisfaction

Florence N. Chukwurah was born to a polygamist family on 25 May 1946 in Onitsha, Nigeria. Her father was a marine engineer. She completed her elementary and high schooling in Onitsha, a city of 1.5 million people, and then graduated in nursing in 1970. Florence married Christopher Chukwurah on 9 November 1974 in Chicago, Illinois, while he was attending the university. They are the parents of three children. On 5 February 1983 Brother and Sister Chukwurah were baptized into the Church. Sister Chukwurah has served as president of the Young Women organization and president of the branch Relief Society.

I grew up in a polygamist home, but there was love in that home. My father had four wives; two had no children. The total number of children from the other two was seven—three from the first wife, four from my mother. I was very attached to my father's first wife, who was much older than my mother. She would often offer me goodies. When I was a very small child, I used to call my own mother "Florence Mother." The way I was brought up, I never knew that she was my mother. I related myself most to my father's first wife. My mother would go to the market in the mornings, but the first wife was available all the time, because she was more or less retired.

My father, a marine worker, was never at home, but always at sea, touring. Whenever he did come, he showed me he loved me very much.

I grew up in a neighborhood where there were many Protestant families. My father, who was baptized a Roman Catholic, became a nonactive member of that church because he married many wives. So we were never baptized as infants.

I did feel a need to join my peer group on Sundays, to worship. On many occasions I attended Catholic churches. Because I didn't understand what was being said, I moved to look for another church, where Ibo was spoken and I could understand what the preacher was saying.

One Sunday I attended the Anglican church with the family of one of my childhood friends. I understood all the preacher said that day, and so I became convinced I should become an Anglican, though I wasn't baptized until I was about ten years old.

I had to work very hard for that baptism. I didn't tell my parents that I wanted baptism; nobody in my family knew what I was doing. I secretly attended catechism, got myself godparents, and then one day ran to one of my mother's younger sisters to tell her I was ready for baptism. She, being an Anglican, was very happy. She bought me a new white dress to wear, and accompanied me. After my baptism, my godparents took me to my mother and announced the baptism. She was a little surprised and very happy that I should carry on such an important assignment without telling her.

I got my first schooling certificate in 1958. I worked very hard for it, because even though my father had a lot of money, he never made investments, so when he retired it came as a surprise to him that he had not saved up much for his children. My family became poor, and I had to work hard.

In standard six [eighth grade], I gained an interest in secondary school, because I was a fairly bright scholar. But when I passed the entrance exam for secondary, my parents couldn't send me because they didn't have enough money. I cried all night and all day. No help came from anybody.

I wrote another exam for a smaller school and passed, but again there was the financial problem. A money lender lent my father some money, and that attracted a lot of interest. My father didn't have a job then, and my mother was only a trader.

I went to school with the borrowed money, but made up my mind that I was going to pay it back when I was through school.

Nursing appealed to me. I loved the look of the uniform, and I had sympathy for sick people. But I didn't know if I could handle the work or if I could stand some of the ugly sights, so I went down on my knees and asked God to help me.

I wrote the exam and passed very well. I attended the Queen Elizabeth School of Nursing in Umuahia, one of the best in Nigeria then.

When I started my nursing career, I had a tough time. Those students with sponsors had it easy. As soon as my allowance started coming in, I started paying off gradually the money my father had borrowed for my two years of secondary school. It took me three years to pay that off. Then I became more free and was able to stand on my own.

I had heard of the law of tithing, and as a girl of sixteen or seventeen, I started paying tithing, though it wasn't a full tithe. We were asked to make a vow of how much we thought we could chip in to the tithing fund. I remember paying five shillings a week from my little allowance. That must really have helped me, because all through those years I had no obstacles, no financial problems. I was even able to help my parents.

In 1965 I sat for my examinations and passed. I received a present from the school of nursing as the best nurse, academically and professionally, of the year. The Bible commentary I was given is still in my home today, and I have showed it to my children.

Then the Nigerian civil war broke out. Although some of my mates were getting married, I didn't want to marry at that time. And sharing a man, as my mother had to, was something I didn't want to put up with. I was bent on having my own husband and my own children to take care of. Even though I had some suitors, I never gave in to any of the young men who wanted to marry me.

My mother and father were separated during the war, and I supported my mother, my only brother, and my two sisters.

After the war, we found my father alive, but he was starving and was very ill, almost to the point of death. He was a devoted Christian, and during the war he always prayed that he would live to see us again, even if he died soon after.

Being a nurse, I could see that he wasn't ill, but was badly starved. My mother and I went to work and gave him all the necessary foods. In no time, he was back on his feet again, feeling very well. He lived for many more years, not dying until May of 1977.

I passed the midwifery exam and returned to Onitsha, because I wanted to marry someone from there. I got a job in St. Charles Borromeo Hospital (it's a Catholic hospital, but I was not discriminated against), where I proved my leadership capabilities and became the director of nursing.

Knowing I was ready for marriage, I started to fast and pray seriously to know the man that would marry me. By then I was a member of the Spiritual church. In my culture, you do not accept a boy-meets-girl marriage. My mother cried when I fasted for three days; but I just told her that I was talking to my Lord so he would give me somebody to marry, especially somebody who didn't drink or smoke.

In a few weeks after those three fasting days, I met my beloved husband, Christopher Chukwurah. He came one afternoon when I was preparing for the Christmas party at the hospital. He approached my cousin Edward Onyejekwe and asked who I was. I could hear somebody talking to Edward. When Edward signaled me, I came out and met a charming, tall, elegant-looking man, who I thought was coming to me for medical advice.

He spoke to me and proposed marriage, the way our culture allows. I looked at him and said, "Well, I will give you an answer later." I wanted to consult Edward, and also my parents.

Christopher didn't even frown, as I expected he would.

When I arrived at the party late (which I never did), my friends asked what made me late. I told them that a man had come along that afternoon and proposed to me, and I was very excited.

I didn't know then whether or not he smoked or drank. A couple of weeks after that, he came back, and I told him I really loved him. I had thought about him and hoped that he was going to be my man.

Soon after, he left for Lagos, but before he left he told his parents that he had found somebody he wanted to marry.

He came back again and again and again. Finally, after two months of courting, his father came to my home to see me and find out who the lady was who was going to wear his son's shoes.

I presented him the traditional cola nut, as we do in our culture. I gave him a chair and told my father that somebody was waiting.

In our tradition, the cola nut is a symbol of love. If somebody visits you and you do not present a cola nut, it appears that you are that person's enemy. The nut is a sign of welcome.

Christopher's father accepted the cola nut but told me that I must also give him water and soap and a towel—which I did. He washed his hands thoroughly before he broke the cola nut. This greatly impressed me, because many men in our culture never do that. He was a neat, very clean, even elegant old man.

After that, he was happy and he left. He invited me to his home, and I visited as many times as I could before Christopher and I were engaged in the traditional manner in March of 1972.

Immediately after our engagement, Christopher traveled, and I was left alone. I had many temptations come my way, but I never succumbed to them. I lived a very strict and chaste life.

After many struggles, I finally obtained a visa to go to Canada, where I could be close to Christopher, who was working in the United States, while I tried to get a visa to join him in America. He paid my fare. I was very pleased. When I arrived, it was a very, very happy day for both of us, after our having stayed apart for two years and four months.

The day before I left, my father gave me a blessing. He placed his hands on my head and said prayers, blessing me that I would have a fruitful married life, that my husband would love me and be a responsible father, and that my family would be blessed. Afterwards, he broke down and cried like a baby. He said he was getting old and I might never come back to meet him alive. I cried. My mother, who was sick with cancer, was not able to see me off.

When I arrived in Ottawa, I got a basement apartment. We tried several times to get me a visa for entering the United States before having our wedding, but failed. One day we were so frustrated we went to the United States consulate and asked what to do. They asked us to enroll for a court marriage, which we did immediately, and we were wed in the court.

The last day before I was to be deported back to Nigeria, I finally got a visa for the United States. I was overwhelmed with joy, as was Christopher. The next week I traveled to the United States and joined my husband. We were more than happy.

We had another wedding, a church wedding, in Chicago. It wasn't very elaborate, because we had so little money, but we were very happy to be joined together in a church.

The day I arrived, my husband had only one dollar left, and we had a rough life, starting out fresh. I didn't know what to do. I was not allowed to work officially, and we had no money to send me to school.

Finally, with some coaching, I sat for my General Education Exam and got ready for a university program in the United States. I got an unauthorized job so we could survive.

Then we had our first son, Chukwuemeka.

Because we were hard working, and we loved each other so much, people around us in Bloomington, Illinois, thought we were millionaires. We never told anybody our problems, only God. When we had problems, we would kneel down and talk to God.

During our stay in the United States, we investigated many churches but, unfortunately, never heard anything about The Church of Jesus Christ of Latter-day Saints. In fact, friends in one of the Protestant churches told us that they would sponsor us to set up their church in Nigeria, but we did not want to get involved.

We decided to go home to Nigeria when I was heavy with our second child. We felt that with two children we would not be able to remain self-supporting students in the United States.

When we again started life back in Nigeria, we had no money. I didn't have a job for five months, and Christopher's income was not very good. But somehow, God was on our side, and we were able to manage. Because we loved one another, we didn't have problems.

Finally I got a job at the general hospital in Aba, and we were able to make ends meet more easily, and also were able to take care of extended-family problems. I had two junior sisters and a brother to support. My husband, being the first in his own family, was supporting his own relatives. My husband and I always got together and decided what to do with our money.

I now have a better job, as head nurse of the clinic at the Federal Government College in Ikot Ekpene, and we have three loving boys. I also have living with me two of my sister's children. My sister's husband died four years ago. We finance these children's schooling and support them completely.

All my life, since childhood, I have had an urge to serve the Lord. Something pushes me to serve—someone, somewhere. In the churches we've belonged to, we have always served to the best of our abilities.

We belonged to a particular church but lost interest because what the people in that church said was not what they did. My husband and I got together and said, "Well, we must ask the Lord what to do now." We prayed and fasted. Then on the thirty-first of December we asked God to show us where to worship. We wanted to find a place where we would have peace, where the doctrines and principles of the church would be what the church members were doing.

After this fast and prayer, we found the Church through our late friend, Brother Apugo. Somehow we had a persistent urge to visit him, and when we met him, he told us about The Church of Jesus Christ of Latter-day Saints.

This man surprised me. When I had known him as a young man, he wasn't religious, and his behavior didn't show any religious inclinations. When he found the Church, he became a changed man. He was able to talk about his church, and we became interested. My husband and I looked each other in the eyes and said, "It looks like the prayer we said a few weeks ago has been answered."

We asked Brother Apugo to take us to the local leader of his church, who then was Brother Ituma. We arrived at eight in the evening. We were told of the Church, we collected a few Church tracts, and then we went home and studied them.

We got hold of a Book of Mormon, because the word *Mormon* originally had frightened me, and I wanted to find out if my fears were justified. I studied it as best I could, and asked God to show me if this really was a true book.

After the prayer, I had peace, which I felt was an answer to my question.

We investigated the Church for three weeks, hurried to receive the lessons, and both decided to be baptized the same day. At the time of my baptism, I felt a spiritual satisfaction—that I had really gotten into the boat that would pilot me, if I lived the life I should. Before that time, I felt that when somebody died, that was it. We have remained very sincere in the gospel.

The things that most impressed me about the Church were the emphasis on family togetherness and the love the missionaries showed to us. The love was the first thing that really caught my attention.

The Church has made it easy for me to appreciate my fellow beings and to keep morning and evening devotions. I tell my children, "Try to do one good thing to a fellow human being today. Then you have achieved something during this day." Our family home evenings, in which we talk and reason things over, make it easy for our children to be very close to us. In fact, the people around us in the college community see my husband and me as an inseparable couple, and they want to find the secret behind our togetherness. We tell them that it's nothing other than The Church of Jesus Christ of Latter-day Saints, which emphasizes the family. Even though my husband and I loved each other and have always been close, we have been even closer since joining the Church. A true Latter-day Saint is seen as a light anywhere he or she is.

Immediately after our baptism, I became the Relief Society president in the Aba Branch. Later, that branch split, and I remained president. Then we got a chapel in Ogbor and gained many good sisters. We had many good times in homemaking meetings, and we showed love to one another.

In 1985, when I had my third baby, my husband, who was the branch president, released me from the Relief Society, so that I would have time to take care of my baby. When I became stronger, I was given another call to be president of the Young Women, a position I held for a year and a half.

I have, through my family life, brought some people to the Church. Many people who would like to investigate the Church have come to me. The problem is that many husbands are difficult and don't want to join their wives; it has been a difficult thing to get husbands to come to church. We have invited such friends to our family home evenings. I am sure that one of these days, the husbands will be moved to join the Church. The sisters in Nigeria struggle to increase their families' incomes; because the cost of living is so very, very high, no one man can make it alone. Our sisters face the ordeal of helping to support the family, whether they are educated or not.

I would like my family to remain faithful, to be dedicated to the gospel, to be honest to themselves, to love each other, and to marry in the Church.

9

Celestine N. Onuka

Nothing Good Comes Easy

Celestine N. Onuka has experienced an unusual life of struggle and trial. These hardships began with the tragic and sudden death of his father when Celestine was a young boy. Yet, his struggles helped him focus his efforts to achieve an education and later to devote his life to being a faithful member and missionary in the Church. Celestine was born on 15 May 1960 in Amuke Ohafia, Nigeria. After a trying and difficult youth, Celestine found the Church and joined it in 1983. He was one of the first, and one of the most successful, full-time missionaries ever to serve in Nigeria.

I am the first son of my father. I was born in a little village in Ohafia, in Imo State. My father was a teacher in the Presbyterian church, one of the pioneers of that church in the area. My mother came from an area in Cross River State.

I was seven years old when my father died. My mother tells me that my father had in mind that I would be an engineer.

My father was to go to the United States to get an education, but the people in our area, because of timidness or something, thought that associating oneself with an American created a talisman [something having magical properties]. This meant that people could go to any other part of the world to get an education, but not to America. They accused my father of associating himself with people who were not good Christians. Eventually he was poisoned by a member of the family. Every day, when he was on his sick bed, I used to lie down with him.

It was not an easy thing for my mother to cope with the loss of my father. It was not easy for me to continue schooling, because my father was the only breadwinner. My mother sold foodstuffs from her farm so I could pay my fees and finish my primary school in December 1973.

I had faith and hope that I would go to secondary school, but I didn't know how I would do it. The greatest difficulty was finding the money for school fees and books. After speaking with the principal, I went home and wept bitterly, because I could not afford it.

I went back and told the principal, "I do not have the money, but I hope to pay it later on." He put my name in and allowed me to go to school. Whenever a teacher would drag me out of the class to expel me, the principal would put me back. Unfortunately, he was posted to another school, and a new principal came in. It became more difficult for me to continue.

Each day I would trek seven miles to school, and then seven miles back home. Because it was so far, I was not able to attend every day. I worked on a farm to earn money for my exercise books and two pens. I would often borrow school books from my friends, because I could not afford to buy them. All that I hoped for was to go to school. I decided that would require sacrifice, so I did what I had to do.

A friend of my father agreed to help me complete my schooling, but after one year he died. Though this was one of the most disheartening things I had to face in my life at this time, I was determined to continue in school.

Sometimes the teachers would ask me about my fees. I used to boldly tell them where my home was and how I managed to walk so far to school and that I didn't want to leave. Some of the teachers would have pity on me; some would say I must go. But I never gave up. Even if I was sent out, I would hang on by the window and listen to the teacher. During break time, I tried to talk to some of the boys who were good to me; I would look through their notes so that I was knowledgeable.

Then, one day it was discovered that the accountant had misused school funds, including money the students had paid. So I said I was among those people who had paid my school fees, but had not been issued a receipt. Since there were so many incidents, the school accepted my word, and I was able to complete that school year.

The next year I had a friend, a girl, who was very good to me. I regarded her as a sister. She did all she could to help me. I was permitted to stay with her family, and she provided food and laundry. At school, I participated in literary groups, debate, and choir. The school was very proud of me. I did not pay school fees that year.

In my final year of school, I left my friend's house, because I felt ashamed to be taking from the family and not contributing. I often slept at the homes of some of my friends who lived near the school, so I would not have to walk home and back. Usually I would not eat with them, so that I wouldn't burden them so much. I lived in that way until I finished school.

It was not easy to take the West African School Certificate exam. I did not know how to pay for it. I had it in the back of my mind that if I could get good grades, then I could make good money. The principal helped me so that I could take the exam.

Usually the results of the exams are released in three months, but when they came out, the school was suspected of malpractice in the examinations—someone had cheated—so all the results were seized. All my hopes were thwarted. I did not know what to do. I had gone for five years to secondary school and not merited anything. I went home and tried to forget my sufferings.

I used to wonder about religion, because of my suffering in my early times, though I was brought up in the Presbyterian church. "Why do all these things happen?" I would ask. This was about 1983.

Especially I wondered about a man called Melchizedek, a king (or high priest) of the most high God who met Abraham returning from the slaughter of the kings (see Hebrews 7). Some ministers said he was Jesus Christ; others said many other things. Many things I tried to find out as a young man made me frustrated. It seemed that there was no true religion.

One day when it was raining, someone came into the quarters where we were trying to dodge the rain. He called out, "Are you one of those people who believe in Joseph Smith and try to talk about it?" The man he had addressed tried to explain something about Joseph Smith and the Book of Mormon, but I know now that he did not know much about the restored gospel.

I became interested. "How can I know more about this thing?"

"We have a missionary who will tell you everything."

"Who?" I asked.

"A white man."

"No. I don't believe all those things. The white men will come and try to tell us many stories."

The missionary did come that evening, though I did not meet him.

The next morning I went up to where the man had directed me to go to hear the message. The missionary came up to me. I said, "I am Celestine. I met one of your members, who introduced a kind of book to me, and I would like to know more about it. But before we go on, let us talk about something I want to know. I want to talk about Melchizedek."

He told me many things about Melchizedek, and these satisfied me. Then he started telling me about the restored gospel. He handed me a copy of the Book of Mormon. I said I would like to read it before we talked about it more.

As a history student, the more I read it, the more interested I became, and before I could meet the missionary again, I had finished the Book of Mormon. I told him I had read it, but he did not believe me. So I told him the names of the different books, and some of the headings to the chapters. Then he believed me.

I told him I would like to join his church and asked him how I should go about it?

He said I needed to have the seven discussions; then I could be baptized. I listened to the discussions and afterwards was baptized.

Very soon after my baptism, I got a job in a nail factory in Aba. One day when I was working, somebody from my village came to me. He said I was needed at home. The disputed land that my father had had, I might be able to get. Some of my uncles, my father's half brothers, had tried to seize this land, and they and my mother had been talking about it for a long time. The man who had bought the undeveloped land had refused to keep it and had asked for his money back. The money was returned to him.

I was living the gospel, and the Sunday after I was ordained into the Aaronic Priesthood, to the office of teacher, I was given that land. That increased my faith, because it was a miracle. It increased my faith, and I continued to work.

One time, I had heard at Port Harcourt some people trying to sing "Come, Come, Ye Saints." I knew it was a song I had learned in the Church, and I knew that no other people would sing it unless they knew the Church. So one Sunday I didn't go to church but went down to Port Harcourt, where I had once lived. I went to see a Mormon family, who, when I introduced myself, received me and afterwards drove me back to Aba.

When I returned I told my friends that there were people in Port Harcourt who were members of the Church. "Why don't we try to go see them?" One of my friends told me there had been a missionary, Elder Lars Bishop, who was in the Aba area.

So we drove there and went out and tried to visit some of those homes. The people explained that after the missionary had left, nobody had come back, and the branch president had gone back to his town.

Because of my interest in the Church, and my work in the ward (teaching the Gospel Essentials class), I had quickly learned all the lessons. So the district president, Obinna, from Owerri, called and interviewed me, and I was set apart as a district missionary. We soon opened a branch in Umuahia. Usually, I would go down with the branch president in Aba, and we would teach the hymns.

Then Calvin Crane and his wife came to run the branch. This family influenced my life greatly. But then things started to become hard. I felt that I was not doing much. I would be sent out to do missionary work in nearby towns, and I continued to supervise the branch in Port Harcourt and teach members on any day I was free. The Cranes worked closely with me to develop the different areas. Then the jobs at the nail factory got disrupted, and workers were laid off.

Brother and Sister Crane were asked to open a branch in Calabar, and they asked me to go there with them. There I met Brother Jude Inmpey, at the University of Calabar, and his family, and Dr. Okure, who had then graduated from Brigham Young University and had organized a job corps. They were the only two members of the Church there. Brother Okure was called to be the branch president.

I worked as a missionary, and within some months, we had seventy-four baptisms. That was very encouraging. With all that growth, missionaries were needed in the West African Mission, with headquarters in Lagos.

Missionary work there was not easy, and it has never been easy. This is an area where people do not like to keep the Word of Wisdom and the law of chastity. So you need to be very cordial in the way you talk to them.

I was the third full-time missionary of the Church in Nigeria. I received a subsidy of twenty-five naira [$3.50] a week. Things were very hard, but that was part of the sacrifice. Also, I had to forget about home, which I loved, and concentrate on my missionary work.

During this time, we baptized up to two hundred people, and there were many others we taught who did not try to join the Church, because of their weaknesses.

Many more missionaries were called, and people from many places were calling President Palmer and asking him to establish the Church in their areas. I worked in many places. In my record, I have seven hundred baptisms from all the places I worked in two years.

In September 1986 I was released from my mission, and I was very happy. I served, though I knew that nothing good comes easy. I was very, very grateful to my Heavenly Father, who provided me with the opportunity to serve him all those days and call all those souls to his kingdom.

In Aba I held a job in the Church as a music director, until the stake was created. At that time I was called to be the first ward clerk in the newly formed Aba First Ward. I am very happy. I know that this church is the only true church upon the face of the earth. I have no shred of doubt in my mind. Things are going to work out fine for me. I still have that hope. I want only to have a steady job and to get married. I myself do not have time for education, but my children will have it.

If I am given a chance to go to school, then I will. But the more I think about it, the more distressed I get, and I don't want people to see me in that mood. They will say, "Is that somebody who says he is worshipping a true God?" I don't want people to think I am attending a church that is not good, and that God is punishing me because I am serving in the wrong church. I want them to look at me and be proud of me.

After my father died, I tried to remember how he loved me, and how he used to be. He didn't like anybody to beat me, and he would give me anything that I wanted. I know other stories about my father, so I know he was a really good man.

It was when I joined this church that I found that my father had a copy of the Book of Mormon, dated 1965, and other handouts. I don't know where he got them. I guess because he had these, people thought he was trying to communicate with people who were not good. I think he was planning to go to school in Utah. After he died, a letter came from the school he was trying to attend, but that letter has since been lost. I would like to know where my father was planning to go to school.

I did use his copy of the Book of Mormon and had it with me for a time. I kept it at home when I went down to Calabar, but when I finished my mission and returned, I did not see it again.

Learning of the Restoration meant the most to me—learning about someone fourteen years old who was interested in religion and Jesus Christ, but who did not know which church he should join. He went to a grove of trees and prayed and saw two personages.

The greatest of all blessings is the authority to do things — to baptize, to work for Jesus Christ. The Restoration and priesthood authority are the greatest things that made me join the Church.

Another great teaching is baptism and other ordinances for the dead. Now that I am older, I realize that my father loves me. I love him. I would like to be with him someday in a family relationship in heaven — something made possible by ordinances of the restored gospel.

One of the things the Church has done is make me feel that if I live better and am content with what I have, I will be happy here on earth and in the life to come. I have a sense of belonging, because the Church has become part of me; members regard me as a brother, so my family is large. I no longer drink palm wine. I have had girlfriends, but I have treated them just like sisters. Chastity was not a problem.

There is nothing so happy as seeing somebody you've taught the gospel go into the waters of baptism. It gave me great joy to see converts stay fast in the Church and grow.

I hope my children and grandchildren will think of their father and grandfather as walking up to the gospel. I was told, and I believed. They will not have to be told, because they are my children. I will help them understand all the principles that have been laid down for us here on earth. If they will keep to the precepts, recognizing all authorities, especially the prophets and the leaders of the Church, they will have a home not only here on earth, but also in the celestial kingdom of glory. If they unite themselves and love one another, they will be blessed.

10

Jude I. Inmpey

The Lord's Hands Upon Me

Jude I. Inmpey, one of the first people in Nigeria to join the Church, was born on 24 July 1927 in Umuori Iho, Nigeria. His life was miraculously spared when he was a boy of six. He studied to be a priest in the Catholic church. After his schooling, he married Angelina Okasi in 1957. She died in giving birth to her eighth child. Brother Inmpey suffered the ravages of a civil war in his country. He married again in 1978; his wife, Mary, has borne six children. In 1979 he was given a pamphlet by a missionary couple and was baptized in July of that year. He has served as a district president and as the first counselor in the Nigeria Aba Mission presidency.

When I was six years old, there was a conspiracy against me; some people were sent to kill me. A man came and fired a gun at me and discharged bullets or pellets into my stomach. This may have been due to personal jealousy toward my father, who died one month before I was born. I was the only male issue of my father, and out of jealousy they wanted to kill me so that he would be without anyone. There was no hospital anywhere nearby that I could be taken to. My mother loved me so much she would have killed herself, if not for people constraining her. After delaying a long time, to know whether I would live or die, one man, seeing my mother grieving, carried me on his shoulders and trekked ten miles to the hospital to get me treated. I stayed there for two weeks, then was discharged.

That is one of the greatest things I remember when I was a child. It was a tragic event. So many things can combine to rob one's life, but God in his infinite mercy can thwart all these things. I can see why the people who wanted to kill me when I was young were not able to do so—the good Lord wanted to provide a way for me to follow him. The devil wanted to take me out of the way so that I could not get the chance to join the Church.

When I was seven years old, my mother died. I was an orphan. I started school but had to drop out because there was no one to pay my school fees.

When I was seventeen years old, I was so depressed because of the condition of my life that I wanted to join the reverend fathers as a priest in the Roman Catholic church. The thought was so heavy in my mind that I approached a reverend father in 1944 and told him that I wanted to become a priest. In 1945 I passed the entrance examination and was sent to the seminary in Onitsha. I was there for five years; I then received the senior Cambridge school certificate and was sent to the senior seminary at Enugu.

In Enugu, the thought came to me that this wasn't the place for me. My desires to be a priest were suddenly gone, and at the time I didn't know why. I went to the bishop and told him that I had an urge to leave the seminary because my mind was telling me that I was in the wrong place. I said, "There are some questions I have been asking, and nobody has been able to give me a good answer for them. What is your advice?" The bishop was a very kind man. He was very understanding. He told me to pray, to do what we called an *obina*, which is to pray for nine consecutive days and then ask God for direction. I did that, and on the ninth day the thought that I should leave was stronger in my mind.

When I told the bishop my feelings, he said he was going to release me, because it might be that God had something else for me to do, and not in that place. He said, "God must have designed you for something in the future, and maybe you'll know it later on." He gave me some traveling money. I went home. That was when I was about twenty-three years old.

When I joined the Church I remembered this experience. If I had not left the seminary, I would not have joined this church. If I had continued, I would have been a reverend father or a bishop by now, and I could have never left to join this church, because I would not have been able to leave what I'd been doing. It was a blessing that I cut off my plans instead of continuing.

Many were not happy when I left the seminary. When I later joined the Church in 1979, they said, "Why did you leave us and go to that one? You could have been a bishop by now in our church." I said, "I would rather not be anything in my church than be a bishop in your church, because I would have lost my way through it. I think God wanted me to join this church, and maybe he also wants you to join the Church, and maybe you would like to join the Church as I have done." It was difficult at that time because people were ridiculing me and cracking jokes at me. But when they see that I am seriously engaged in it, they begin to wonder if there is really something there.

Eventually I went to Lagos to find work. I found a job there as a clerk in the Accountant General Department. For eighteen months I was in this ministry, but not feeling comfortable with the clerical employment, I resigned the appointment in 1952 and secured employment as a technical officer in training with the Posts and Telecommunications Department in Lagos. From 1952 to 1956 I received training as a telecommunication technologist at the Ministry Technical School at Oshodi, Lagos. In 1962 I was sent to England, where I studied with the British Post Office School at Stone, England. I had my industrial attachment training with the Creed and Company Telegraph Equipment School in Croyden, England, and with the Siemens Telegraph School in Munich, West Germany. I worked with the Posts and Telecommunications Department till May 1986, when I retired from the Federal Service. While working there I married Angelina Okasi, who gave me eight children, five of whom are still alive. My wife died during childbirth in 1966. After the death of my wife, everything seemed to have come to a dead stop. I loved my wife, and there was nobody to look after the children who were still very tender—the oldest was about nine years old.

During this time the Nigerian civil war was raging. We began running from place to place, with no place to hide ourselves. The planes were dropping bombs here and there, and there was no food to feed my five children. There was nothing to do except to pray to God to give us sustenance. By the grace of God we all survived the war; none of the children died.

Our family suffered tremendously. First, there was no food. Second, there was no money. I was a civil servant still, but at the end of the month I couldn't get my salary. If I got a check, I couldn't get money from the bank, because there was no money in the bank. If my check was twenty pounds, I would go to the bank and only get five pounds, because there was not enough cash. If I got the five pounds home, I could not buy a meal because the cost of food was very high. There were times we would go without food, and we'd have to go into the bush and collect vegetables and boil them and mix them with pawpaw [papaya] and pineapple. I couldn't farm, because what I farmed the soldiers would destroy. They would reap the food before it was ready for reaping. Moreover, we didn't know where we would be the next season, because people migrated from place to place. We started in Enugu and moved south until we had covered about 150 kilometers in order to run away from the Nigerian soldiers. As we went, we thought we had escaped death, but in about a month or so, the soldiers would appear near us, and we'd have to run again. We continued running until we ran home to my village, and there we stayed. The war ended in January 1970.

During the war years I wanted to join the army to help to fight. But the more I determined to enter the army, the more the army would not take me. They were enlisting people older than myself, but they wouldn't take me. It was strange to me that I was not accepted into the army. But now I look back and I feel that my experience during the Nigerian civil war is another instance of the Lord's hands upon me. So many people joined the army and never came back. Maybe I would have been killed and wouldn't have got the chance to do the things I'm doing now, like going to the temple of the Lord. I think God knows the best.

From 1975 to 1978 my mind was diverted by trying to read the scriptures. I was very much interested in scriptural things, because I wanted to find out the reason why things are. I read the scriptures as much as I could, but I couldn't gather much.

Then I started researching churches. I borrowed library books dealing with various church units. What I was really looking for, I didn't know, but I was searching and reading and trying to coordinate something, but I couldn't pinpoint what it was. I continued going to the Catholic church, and was attending the normal services when time would permit, but one thing was prominent in my mind: during the war years I had thrown away my rosary. Why I had done so, I didn't know. I refused to say the beads anymore. Instead, I just started praying, doing personal prayers or reading the psalms. I didn't see the sense in counting beads or repeating prayers. But I was still attending church.

One day in May 1979 I went to the insurance office, where I met two elderly couples. They were distributing pamphlets to the insurance agent, and I wanted to have some. When they said it was about religion, I was very interested because I was trying to find out something I didn't know. They gave me some of the pamphlets. I asked them, "What type of religion is this?" They told me, "The

Church of Jesus Christ of Latter-day Saints." I said, "Oh, this is one of the other churches again. Who gave you authority to teach the gospel? How did you get it?" They told me that if I would like to know, they would tell me how they got the authority. I said, "Well, I am interested. I would like to know what you are talking about, and I will come and argue with you. I am sure I will defeat you in my argument, because I have done so with other churches, who then ask me to come and teach for them. Where do I meet you?"

They gave me an address. I went there and was introduced to Elder Mabey and Elder Martin. They told me about The Church of Jesus Christ of Latter-day Saints, and I was curious because I had so many questions which nobody had been able to give me the answers to. I asked them a question, and they answered, opening the Bible and showing me the place in the Bible. I said, "Wonderful." I asked another one, and they gave me another instance in the scriptures. I said, "But I've been reading the scriptures all along. Why didn't I see the answer?" I said, "Have you some pamphlets?" They said, "Yes." They gave me *Which Church Is Right? The Plan of Salvation,* and other pamphlets. *Which Church Is Right?* is sort of a historical background about the early churches. That was easy for me, because I had studied church history and I knew that what they were talking about was true. That wasn't a problem at all, but the other ones were a bit new to me, and I did not fully comprehend them. After reading the pamphlets, I wanted more books. I was given the Book of Mormon to read. I hungrily and hurriedly read it. It took me about a day or two. Then I said I wanted something more that would be historical and scriptural, something doctrinal that would let me know the difference between their teachings and the teachings of other churches. Then the brother gave me *Gospel Principles,* and I read it. It made a lot of sense to me.

I attended church for six weeks. One day, Elder Mabey asked me, "Inmpey, what is holding you back from being baptized?" I said, "Baptism again? I've been baptized before." He said, "No. That baptism was not enough. You have to be baptized again." I said, "Where does it say that?" Then after our discussion I was convinced that I had not had a good baptism after all, because it was by sprinkling, and it should be by immersion. Also, it had to be done by the proper authority. The next Sunday my wife and I were baptized. The following Sunday one of my sons was baptized.

I had taken some time before I agreed to be baptized. I wanted to be sure. I knew if I joined the Church my family would follow me, and I didn't want to lead them astray and then take them out again. It would be a mistake to leave the Catholic church to join another church and then turn around and leave that new church; they would think that I was stupid. I wanted to be absolutely sure that this was the true Church, and that is why I delayed. When I got baptized, I had no regrets whatsoever.

I can't say that I had a hundred percent assurance of what I was doing at the time of my baptism, but I had a belief that what I was doing was right. As time went on, I developed a full understanding, and I fully comprehended, and now I thank my stars for the day I made that decision to be baptized.

Ten days after my baptism, Elder Mabey called me and said, "Inmpey, we'd like to make you an elder." I said, "What does that mean?" He explained it to me, and I said, "Well, if that is the Church system, I would like to be made an elder." Two months after that, Elder Mabey said, "Brother Jude, we'd like to make you the district president." I asked, "What is the district president?" He said, "You'll be in charge of the Owerri District." I said, "Okay, if that's the system in the Church, I'll take the office, but I don't know what to do." He said, "You'll be taught." So I was made the district president. That was in 1979. Then, in 1981 I was called as the first counselor to President Espensheid, the first mission president in Nigeria. From that day until 1986, the next four mission presidents called me to be their first counselor.

In March 1987 the mission president said, "How would you like to work with the mission records, to put them in order?" I said, "Well, I'll try to do my bit and see what I can do." Since then I have been working full-time trying to finalize the records. I went to England for some training and, while there, had the opportunity to go to the temple of the Lord and get endowed.

The greatest blessings of all the blessings that I can so far record are completing my genealogy, being sealed to my parents, and completing my own sealing and endowment in the temple. I had to struggle to make sure that I did the genealogy and temple work for my parents. I struggled hard to get it done. The day I had done it and had been sealed to my parents, I was the happiest man on earth.

I think that the greatest of all the gifts I have received so far is the opportunity I had to go to the temple of the Lord. I think it is one of the things I have prayed for during all these times. It is miraculous I had the chance to do so.

When I entered the temple, it was the most spectacular thing I could ever behold, because I could hardly believe not only the beauty of it but also that the ceremonies and what took place there were all so highly spiritual. We spent much time there. I wish I could remain there forever and ever and not come out. It was a bother to have to come out of the temple after the first session.

Sometime around 1986 I had a dream. At the time it was happening, it seemed as if it was real life, but then I woke up and found that it was all a dream. I could not understand it. I forgot all about it until months later, when the mission president invited me to attend a gathering. I found that I was the only black person there. I was asked to make some comments, and I remembered my dream, and I saw its meaning clearly. It was like a revelation, but it was down to a level that was easy for me to understand. I said, "I had a dream which happens to synchronize us in this situation. This is a gathering and everybody here, except me, is white—I am the only black person. It seems that this very day has already been foreseen and given to me in a dream. In my dream, I found myself in a very big gathering with many white people. There was music coming from an organ, but for some reason the music didn't seem to be pleasant. Many people were shouting, 'What is wrong with your music?' Then someone answered, 'Look, he's only playing the white keys and not the black ones.' All of a sudden the person playing the organ corrected this and started playing the music by combining the white and the black keys. The melody was restored and everybody was happy." Then I said to the mission president and the others at the gathering, "For many, many years the Church has been playing only the white keys, but now we are playing on the white and the black keys, and the music is much, much sweeter."

Reflecting back, I think I can bear my testimony that I have sometimes wasted time in the past, and I thank God for the day that I met Elder and Sister Mabey, which led me to become a member of the Church. I think that was the most glorious day in my life. I bear my testimony that The Church of Jesus Christ of Latter-day Saints is the true church. It is manifested in many ways: by what we read, by what we feel personally and individually, in our homes, in our actions, and in our lives.

My life has changed tremendously since I accepted the gospel. It would take a long time to tell details, but one aspect that really thrilled me was the Word of Wisdom. Before I joined the Church, I drank and smoked and did all sorts of things, and that was really affecting my health. But when I learned of the Word of Wisdom and stopped drinking tea and coffee and alcohol, it strengthened me. It made me seem to be nearly twenty years younger. I could feel it in my body. Without taking medications, I was able to feel stronger.

I think the Church has given me the idea of what family life should be. I have changed tremendously as a father and as a husband in that now we do things together. We hold our family home evening together, we instruct the children in the way of the gospel, and we say our prayers together. The children are growing up with a knowledge of the gospel, while before we had no time for such things. In the churches we used to belong to, the instruction was given by the reverends or the catechists. Parents had no responsibility to train their children. Now we know that to train our children and bring them up in the knowledge of the Lord are the responsibility of our family. We know about the eternal nature of the family, whereas before it was "until death do you part." Now we know we will meet after death, and in eternity we'll be a family again if we struggle hard to do what we're told. This is sort of a nurturing stage, in which we can build our family so we can continue hereafter. This principle is a motivator to make us do things well, because we know we will meet again hereafter.

I find it a pleasure to serve as a Church worker and as a Church officer. Any office at all in the Church is a pleasure to me. Now that I know the gospel, I will work until I can't work anymore, and I will give anything, even my life, to see that this work goes on. It is really a challenge, but I know it is true.

I bear my testimony that Joseph Smith was a prophet of God and is a prophet today. We have a living prophet—Ezra Taft Benson. The Church of Jesus Christ of Latter-day Saints is the true and divine church of God on earth. If we follow the teachings of the Church and do all the ordinances, from the beginning to the end of our lives, I think life will be sweet. Sure, there will be hardships in life, but we will not mind them so much, because we will know that we are following in the footsteps of our Lord and Savior, Jesus Christ. This will give us joy, and we'll conquer most of our problems on earth.

11

Baende L. E. I. Isekuncola

I Had Been Searching for God

Baende L. E. I. Isekuncola was born on 12 October 1934 in Basankusu, Zaire. He was reared in Kinshasa, the capital city of Zaire, which has a population of about 3.5 million. In 1958 he married Botonca Ilinga; they are the parents of five children. After graduating from the university in Paris, France, Brother Isekuncola returned to Zaire, where he has worked for thirty-six years as a personnel manager. He joined the Church in January 1988 after much searching and study.

I was born in 1934 of parents who started out as pagans. My father later joined the Catholic church and was a sacristan, the person who helps the priest get things ready for meetings and helps clean the building.

When I was small, my parents divorced. I stayed with my father, but visited my mother. Later I went to live in Kinshasa with my paternal uncle. This is a normal custom in my culture. A child belongs to society. Whether I lived with my father or mother, or an aunt or uncle, it was all the same thing.

I did all my studies, grade school and high school, in Kinshasa. I married in 1958.

After the independence of my country, there was in 1962 a test to see who would study in France. I passed and was among the candidates who went to France, where I studied for three years. My specialty was telecommunications.

I have worked for the government as a civil servant. Recently I was called to the cabinet of the First Commissioner to the State, to work as a personnel chief.

I learned of the Church in 1984, when I read a small book whose author praised the Mormon church because it is one of the rare churches in the world which practices tithing as it ought to be practiced. I felt I had to learn what the believers in this church did to be prosperous, and how they applied the law of tithing.

In 1987 I became so preoccupied with this question that I went to the American Cultural Center here in Kinshasa to get the address of the Mormon church, so that I could write and get exact information. Meanwhile, one of my Christian brothers, a member of the International Way, met the Mormon missionaries in Kinshasa and told me about them. I didn't believe him, because I felt the Church could not yet be in Zaire. I prepared to send my letter to the United States.

Then, one day while talking with my son (my second child) about the word of God, he told me that if I wanted to meet those brothers, I could, since the Church had been established in Kinshasa. I had seen the sign of The Church of Jesus Christ of Latter-day Saints, but had no idea that this church was the Mormon church. The sign impressed me, because it was so well written. I knew that this was a serious Church, not a common one.

One Saturday afternoon I went to get information. I found a brother and asked if I could talk to the missionaries. I thought they lived at the church. He advised me to come on Sunday, when I would be able to meet the missionaries.

I could not do so at that time, because I was a preacher in several churches and had to go each Sunday to preach. So I came on a Tuesday afternoon, 10 November 1987, and had the honor of meeting the Hutchings, who received me well. I had a marvelous contact with them. I only wanted to know how to apply the law of tithing so that I could enjoy the blessings of God, but certain scriptures they showed me struck me, especially Doctrine and Covenants 42:11, "Again I say unto you, that it shall not be given to any one to go forth to preach my gospel, or to build up my church, except he be ordained by some one who has authority, and it is known to the church that he has authority and has been regularly ordained by the heads of the church."

When I read this passage, I was completely shaken. I had been a preacher, but then I asked myself, "Who gave me authority to preach? Who gave me power to preach the word of God?" I had just started to preach because the pastor of a charismatic religious group had asked me to. No one had given me any sort of authority at all. I was eloquent, so I continued to preach. It helped me better learn the word of God, because I read it every day.

The second point that got my attention was Doctrine and Covenants 84:19, which refers to the Melchizedek Priesthood: "And this greater priesthood administereth the gospel and holdeth the key of the mysteries of the kingdom, even the key of the knowledge of God."

That was like a bolt of lightning, because I had had many difficulties in the course of my life, but I had always maintained a dynamic belief. I knew the word of God was true, because God cannot lie. So if I had difficulties, the problem must lie with me. That is why I attended many churches, as a faithful member or to preach —because I was looking for God. So this verse told me what I had been searching for for a long time. Till that time, the priesthood had meant absolutely nothing to me, because I had never been instructed in its importance and real value. I now desired to receive the blessings described in this verse of the Doctrine and Covenants.

During my discussions with President Hutchings, he gave me a copy of the Book of Mormon. I read it several times. He also had a copy of the Doctrine and Covenants, but I could not take it home with me. Finally he gave me permission to take it for one week, and I read the whole book four or five times during that week. I learned many interesting things that I had never known or heard.

I had been searching for God. Because I knew I was a child of God, I couldn't live in misery. That was not possible. When I saw that my life was not that of a child of God, I said to myself that I must find God in order to escape that life. I wanted to see and know God. I wanted him to speak to me; I wanted to hear his voice. I wanted him to tell me why I had difficulties, and what I had to do to overcome them.

After I retired and was without work, we often did not have enough food for the family. My children were falling ill and were threatened with rickets. My wife lost about twenty-five pounds because she was eating almost nothing. If we did get something to eat, we contented ourselves by giving it to the children. I had to sell everything I had in the house, so that we could live. I even put my house up for sale, so that with the money from the house I could orient my life in a different direction and live in another way.

These are the reasons that impelled me to search for and come into the Church. I had read that God always reveals himself to those who search. I knew that God would manifest himself to me one way or another, and help me overcome this difficulty. I was baptized on 9 January 1988 and ordained a priest on 6 March. God has blessed me extraordinarily, in ways that I never expected. It is marvelous that I found what I had searched for, and I can never let it go.

I know that God loves me and answers my prayers. My one desire is to receive the Melchizedek Priesthood. I have a large family, and when they are sick, or my neighbors are sick, I can pray for them, but I cannot lay hands on their heads and bless them because I do not have that authority.

One very interesting thing about my father is that he knew the history of his family. When I visited him in 1951 during vacation, my father gave me the descent of his ancestors for four generations. This is marvelous because, unlike many Africans, I know my genealogy. All my many children are proud that they know their genealogy.

My calling to work for the cabinet has been a blessing. In the public sector where I had worked, retirement is almost like a punishment because it is so complicated. So the new job was truly a blessing from God. He answered my prayers; he did not leave me. The First Commissioner recalled me because he knew me and my capabilities personally, having been my boss before I retired. He pitied me and recalled me.

Let God be praised! I am not in heaven, but neither am I in hell.

I have not had much experience in the Church yet. You might say I am "in gestation," still studying and accumulating understanding. I do know that since baptism and my first priesthood ordination, all the blessings have come.

The largest change in me has been to learn to fear God in the scriptural sense. I am a man, and thus I might commit sin without desiring to. But now, because I revere God, I actively avoid sin, since it is an act of ingratitude to offend God after everything that he has done for me.

Also, there is now complete harmony between my wife and me. There is peace in my home with my children. In fact, my most "turbulent" child was baptized just last week.

I did not ask my wife to become a member of the Church, nor my children, because the scriptures say we must not force. My wife came in spontaneously, from seeing my transformation. She felt I was on the right path. Two of my children came timidly at first but afterwards saw that it was good, and so they stayed. I feel that it was my transformation that drew them to the Church.

Above all, I love to teach the word of God. I wish to receive the Melchizedek Priesthood so that I will be better armed to teach the gospel of Jesus, and so that I can lay hands upon the sick.

God does exist, and without him we have no life. I declare in the name of Jesus Christ that this church is true. I try to live the marvels of the word of God, as they are taught. That which we read in the holy books is true. This is a great testimony to me.

12

Mbuyi Nkitabungi

Something Touched Me ...It Was the Spirit

Mbuyi Nkitabungi was one of the first from his native land of Zaire to join the Church. In the short time he has been in the Church, Mbuyi has served as a full-time missionary to England, as a branch mission leader in Belgium, and —although he is not yet married—as a branch president in Kinshasa, Zaire. President Nkitabungi was born 19 October 1959 in Luebo, Kasai Occidental, Zaire. In Brussels, Belgium, he completed his public schooling. After investigating the Church in Brussels, he was baptized in 1980. He learned the English language on his mission and currently serves as a translator.

I was born in 1959, during the trouble just before the independence of my country. After the trouble, my parents and I came to Kinshasa to live. I was very sick when I was young, maybe because of the climate, but perhaps also because of the conditions I lived in.

My father was a wealthy businessman, trading clothes and clothing material. He was also a polygamist, with two wives and fifteen children. He had no religion, not even a pagan religion. He was like most people in our society today—they may go to church, but it doesn't mean anything to them. My mother is Presbyterian, and we children used to go to church with her every Sunday. She wanted us to be clean and well dressed, and she didn't want us to play soccer on Sunday—which is what I used to do at that time.

In 1969 my father sent me to Belgium to get my education. I succeeded in my education and had a wonderful experience. It was there, in May of 1980, that I had my first contact with the Church.

I was living in an apartment in Brussels, and the missionaries rang the bell. I came down to the door, and the missionaries introduced themselves. There were about five missionaries at the door; they were doing district proselyting, I think. They had just met my twin brother in the park, but he wasn't interested in their message. But I accepted the discussions, though I can't remember exactly why. I only remember that I was interested just in talking with them.

They introduced the Church and talked about the Restoration, and also the testimony of Joseph Smith. They gave me a copy of the Book of Mormon to read, but I told them I didn't like reading.

The things that impressed me most were the First Vision and the plan of salvation. These were things the other churches didn't teach. So when I heard of the story of the First Vision, I said to myself, "Why not? If God revealed himself to prophets before, why not today?" I felt good about that doctrine, and I also felt good about the Word of Wisdom. I had just set a goal to quit drinking the beer we used to have after a soccer game.

I read sections from the Book of Mormon, and felt good about what I read.

When I went to church, the people were very kind to me. I have never experienced discrimination in the Church. That is one of the differences I saw in the Church.

After the discussions, a missionary challenged me to be baptized on 30 June, but when the date came, I refused. Then, from time to time, something touched me—I think it was the Spirit. So, suddenly I had the desire to review the discussions, learn more about the Church, and gain a testimony. I was baptized on 19 July 1980.

I remember that day. It was in the morning, and I was the only one to be baptized in the Brussels Ward. A counselor in the bishopric spoke, saying that life on this earth is very short compared with the complete line of time in the eternities. So our life is like a period. I think he meant that we don't have much time to live here on earth, and so we've got to be obedient and prepare to meet God.

When I returned home after the baptism, I was lying on my back, and a warm feeling came into my chest. I cannot describe the feeling, but I can testify that it was the Holy Ghost telling me that I had made the right decision in getting baptized that day. It was a wonderful, peaceful feeling.

Now I can say without a doubt that The Church of Jesus Christ of Latter-day Saints is the only true church on earth; and since the day of my baptism, I have tried my best to bring my brothers and friends into the Church.

I used to give them pamphlets or copies of the Book of Mormon. I also invited my twin brother to a fireside once, and he enjoyed the subject—the three degrees of glory.

A year later, we returned to Zaire for holidays. I told everyone that I had joined the Church, and some people came to me and wanted to know more about it. So I explained how the Church was restored, and also how I gained my testimony.

Just before I returned to Zaire, my bishop asked me to think about going on a full-time mission. I told him I would give him my answer just after the vacation. During my vacation, I thought a lot about it, wondering how I would have enough money but feeling that the Lord would help me do it. I felt the Spirit strongly and thought the Lord was trying to encourage me to go on my mission.

So I returned and told the bishop of the Brussels Ward that I had decided to accept a call. He was excited, as were some of the members. I filled out some papers and had my interview at the end of October 1981, received the Melchizedek Priesthood on the twenty-fifth of October, got my patriarchal blessing in January, had my interview with my stake president, and received a response from the First Presidency in April. President Spencer W. Kimball sent me to the England Birmingham Mission.

It was hard to convince my mother, father, and brothers that it was necessary for me to go on a mission for the Church, but just before I left, my dad called me on the phone from Kinshasa and told me he would support me.

This was the first time for me to learn the English language, and it took about three or four months to learn it. When I first arrived, I memorized all the discussions in English, and also some scriptures. That is how I came to learn the language. No one taught me a word; I learned everything myself. I learned a lot from my mission: how to teach people, how to live with foreigners, how to be patient, how to be humble.

I became a district leader. I am proud to say that I had about twenty-four baptisms on my mission. I'm not bragging, but missionary work is very hard in Europe. God wanted to help me, so he blessed me with those baptisms, and I was glad to bring the gospel to those people. They needed it, and I know it is the best thing they can get in life, because the Church helps people become better people.

When I returned to Belgium, I became the ward mission leader for the Brussels Ward. I was even called on a one-month mission to help teach missionaries how to be effective. My experience in England helped me in this calling.

Because of visa problems, I returned to Zaire in April 1985. Two days after my arrival, I met Brother Bowcutt, an American Latter-day Saint at the American embassy. He was quite surprised to see me, since I was a member of the Church and was speaking English. I explained my mission to England and told him of my situation in Kinshasa. He invited me to his home later, and we had a good chat. I also met his wife and family.

In early 1986, some Church leaders from the United States came and began to try to establish the Church in Zaire. They had met with President Mobutu of Zaire, a government authority who is a friend of the Church.

I tried to guide the Church leaders, helping them get to know more people in Kinshasa, and get to know the city better, along with the customs and habits of the people. We had a Sunday School and sacrament meeting at the place where I used to live then, and I would translate into French what the English-speaking brother would say. That's how I learned to be a translator.

Eventually we had two families working with us: the Bowcutts, who spoke French; and a family from Utah, the Craguns, from the embassy.

They introduced the gospel to my family. My father and mother attended the first meeting we had in my house. Some members of my family have joined the Church, but some not yet. I pray that they will all become a part of the Church, because it will aid them to be better people, and also help us to do our genealogy work more effectively.

I was quite happy to learn that the Church would be established in Zaire. In 1981, when I came to Kinshasa on vacation, and as people were interested in learning more about the Church, I would tell them that the Church would be established in five years. And in 1986 the Church *was* established in Zaire. That was sort of prophetic.

I am grateful for those people who worked to establish the Church in Kinshasa, because I know what a blessing it will be for my country, and for the people in Zaire.

The Church bought a building in Limité, and I was called as first counselor in the branch presidency. The missionaries have been successful in both teaching and baptizing. They don't have to go knocking on doors as they do in Europe and the United States. People come to the missionaries. The people in Zaire want to know more about the Church because it is new to them. As we testify that it is the only true Church, and as they read the Book of Mormon, they find that the teachings of the Church are the best teachings they have ever heard—doctrines we show them during our discussions, which they haven't found in the Bible. They are quite amazed about the knowledge we have in the Church, and also the books the authorities of the Church have written. They are impressed that the members live what they teach, and that they really believe what they claim to believe. That is quite impressive!

I think that if the people of Zaire live the principles of the gospel, as members do in other parts of the world, our country will be blessed and become better in social ways.

I learned during my mission that when we bring the gospel to a poor family, we can expect that in a few months the family will be better off. The Lord will bless them because they are obedient to the commandments.

In May of 1987 I was called as president of the Limité Branch. The Binza Branch was divided from it. I have learned many things from being a branch president among my people. Most of the members are new converts that come from different religious backgrounds, and they come with their own ideas. I have to help them learn the Church ways of life. We leaders have to help them learn to leave old habits and get the new habits of the Church.

It is really a challenge to be a branch president, particularly here in Kinshasa. The Sunday after my calling as branch president, when I came through the gate at the Limité Branch chapel, I was about to cry. I didn't understand my feelings, but as I looked back to the time when the Brussels Ward was divided and a new bishop was put in, I remembered that when he was worried about something, he would cry. Then I understood my feelings.

Also, in Europe we would have a baptism every week, or maybe once or twice a month. Here in Kinshasa we had over thirty people baptized in one month, and I had to find the time to interview all these new members. Right now, the branch president of the Binza Branch and I are interviewing only the candidates for the Aaronic Priesthood, because we haven't the time to do interviews with other new members. Then we have to interview all who have new callings. There is so much to do that it would take me a full day just to describe it all.

But the Church is true, and the missionaries are doing a divine work here in Zaire. If the Church could send us more couples, more missionaries to help start the Church, that would relieve some of the weight on the shoulders of the branch presidents. What we need most right now is to train members, not bring in more converts. We know that souls are of great worth in the sight of God, but we need well-trained members, so that if we need to split some branches, there will be good leaders in the new branches. Then will come the time to start bringing in more members. We need time to meet with all the new converts, and we need to find callings for them.

I am not married right now, and it requires a lot of money and work to arrange a wedding. So I cannot afford to marry right now, but perhaps next year I will be able to, and after that, go to the temple. In the meantime, I spend most of my time with the missionaries, helping them with translating or guiding them in their work, and helping my family become better acquainted with the Church. My twin brother was close to joining the Church, but for some reason he doesn't want to join right now. He has told me that if he ever does join a church, it will be this one, because its members live what they believe, and he is also impressed by the teaching and doctrines presented at the conferences. When I first returned to Zaire, I had a hard time talking about the Church to other people, but my brother encouraged me and opened the way.

My mother likes the Church. One of her goals was to have a child who became a medical doctor, and one who became a pastor. She sees me as the pastor.

The change in my life has impressed my family and also some of my friends. I can say that because I joined the Church, I have not got as many friends as I used to, because I live a gospel life that they don't live.

13

Adjei Kwame

Now I Was at Home

Adjei Kwame was born and raised in Ghana, studied mechanical engineering for seven years in the Soviet Union, where he completed a master's degree, and then went to Zimbabwe to teach. Through promptings from some remarkable dreams, he found and joined the Church in May 1988. Adjei was born on 14 June 1952 in Duayawa-Nkwanta, Ghana. He grew up in Kumasi, Ghana, where he completed his public schooling and a five-year diploma at Kumasi Polytech.

I was born in a village called Duayawa-Nkwanta, in Ghana. When I was about four, my parents moved to the big city of Kumasi.

As children in a rural area, we were expected to get up each morning and wash our faces. In cleaning our teeth we had to get a stick from the *plantine* [a soft wood] and then beat it hard on charcoal. This would fray the end so we could use it to clean our teeth. Then we fetched water to wash ourselves, plus water for our father, who washed to go to work, and water for our mother, who washed to go to the market.

In the African culture, the family is often very large. When we were young, our parents didn't normally associate with us. Our grandparents had more time for us than they had had for their own children. They spent time teaching us and telling us stories. When we visited my grandmother in the village, we would go with her to the farm, and she would tell us the family history. She would show us the boundaries of the farm so that when we grew up we would know where they actually were. Our grandparents like to talk more to their grandsons than to their granddaughters.

My grandmother also taught us which house [family] we could not marry into. She told us the history of that people—their behavior, deaths, sicknesses, and so forth. She said, "Don't go there. That is evil." Fathers and mothers don't know anything. It's the grandmother who knows everything. If there is any deadlock, say in making a decision, we say we are going to ask our grandmother. She is all-wise. In our culture she is considered to be the greatest. Up to the age of five, I spent most of my time with my grandmother.

My grandmother was a Christian. We would wake up about five in the morning to go to church. It would be very, very awkward for any of us not to go to church on Sunday. She saw that we would lead Christian lives.

I attended school at the Qui Anglican Primary School. Then I went to a technical college. At school I was actively involved in the Red Cross. I was also an officer in the Boys' Brigade, where I trained boys from ages seven to eighteen. It is like the Boy Scouts. I was very active in the Presbyterian church.

When I graduated from the polytechnic school, I was awarded a scholarship to go to the Soviet Union to study mechanical engineering. I arrived in the Soviet Union on 3 September 1976. That was my first experience of cold weather. I was very, very cold. I was not used to dressing up and putting on piles of clothes. I had to adjust to this because it was very cold. I also sweated a lot when I went straight from the cold outside to the hot inside.

When we arrived in the Soviet Union we were taken straight from the airport to a hotel, where we had to undergo certain medical examinations. Then we were taken to our colleges to start learning the language, because without knowledge of the language it was impossible to study in the Soviet Union. It took about ten months to learn the language, and it was very difficult. Then after a two-month break, we started our actual course in mechanical engineering.

We were not isolated from the Russians; we were among them. Each student was given a holiday allowance, so we could actually travel to places. Normally those vacations were planned by the school so that the excursions helped with our studies. I visited many places in Russia.

Soviet buildings look the same, because they are built by the same construction firm, which is all over Russia. There was nothing new to see except meeting different people. Some were not willing to talk to us, but some were very willing to express their feelings about the Soviet government. But they would do this while looking behind them to see if anyone was listening. In general, I would say the Soviet people are a very kind people. They are not violent, as some people might think.

At school we had very good professors. In the Soviet Union there is no absenteeism in colleges. You have to be in class. Classes start at eight and close at two thirty. In every hostel there is a school nurse and a doctor resident to whom you have to report. If the doctor feels that you can't go to school, then you have a leave. But that leave will mean going to the hospital for hospitalization.

The lecture requirements were very strict. We were to present all assignments right on time. Any failure to do this could actually lead to dismissal. I knew of two foreigners and five Russians who were dismissed and sent home. We went to school from Monday to Saturday, so we had only Sunday free.

I was also involved in social groups and volunteer work. I have a very good voice, so I was involved in singing in theaters and attending concerts. I also gave lectures at primary and high schools, telling students about myself and Ghana and how I felt about the Soviet people and nation. As they liked people singing in their own language, I would sing songs in Russian. The language was the barrier. I would have to work about four to six hours extra, after school hours. That is because sometimes I would have to go through dictionaries, trying to find meanings of words that I didn't understand very well.

Because Russia is a one-party state and the party controls everything, the students have to attend political lectures. You can escape going to lectures on physics, mathematics, mechanical and technical drawing, or other such subjects, but not philosophy, scientific communism, or history of the communist party. Any attempt to do this can lead to the expulsion of a student.

Since I was actively involved in the Presbyterian church in Ghana, when I went to the Soviet Union I also wanted to attend church services. There was no Presbyterian church, but there were the Eastern Orthodox and the Baptist churches. People who want to get to church have to travel very far away from the city center, because almost all the churches are out of the city. The churches that are in the city are mostly like museums, where you can go and look at things, such as art.

On every holiday I would travel to some of the European cities. I have been in Germany, Holland, Belgium, France, Finland, Czechoslovakia, Bulgaria, Romania, and Italy. I like to see how people live, and see their culture. Most of the time I spent walking and looking at places. I will go anywhere to see how people actually live. We had little money. We would sleep in railway stations. People were kind to us. Some would take us to their homes for a night.

After passing all my exams, I was given fifteen weeks to write a thesis on a topic which the professors chose for me. I had to solve an actual problem. It was not something abstract. My topic was to modify an existing mechanical workshop by increasing its production and efficiency. I was to find means of increasing the production from 250,000 to 400,000 without changing the machinery. I received an excellent mark and defended the thesis very well. After seven years, I was now qualified as a mechanical engineer with a master's degree.

I found that it was very difficult to get a job in Africa after graduating with a master's degree in mechanical engineering. So when I finished I left for England. But I didn't want to stay in Europe. I had something to do in Africa. As the Zimbabwian government was looking for high school teachers, I came to Fletcher High School near Gweru in June 1984. It is a boys' boarding school with about fifteen hundred students and about fifty teachers.

When I came back to Africa I was thinking in Russian. I found communication very difficult. When a question was asked, my answer came in Russian.

As a child in Ghana I was baptized in the Presbyterian church — I don't remember when. I was told I was baptized. I used to go to church. I liked singing, so I started singing in a choir at the age of nine.

I have always been searching for the truth and the true church. When I went to the Soviet Union, I wanted to go to church and pray all the time. I used to visit churches, even though my professors would actually caution me against that. I kept going. But after a while there was no time to go, because the time was planned in such a way that I wouldn't have the time to go to church.

When I came to Zimbabwe I was not going to a church at all. Then in February of 1988, I kept having dreams about a church building. It looked like a big temple with tall spires or tall towers around it. I would see people dressed in white, and they would be marching to the building. I would stand somewhere far away, looking at them. They were in white robes, not in suits, but in long robes which actually ended at their feet. All the time, they were marching to the building. I wanted to find out what this was that kept coming into my dreams.

I knew that you could have a dream when you had thought of something. But I had never thought of that church. It was not in my thoughts. It never entered my thoughts that I should become a member of that church.

One day as I traveled through Kwe Kwe on my way to Harare, I saw a church building of The Church of Jesus Christ of Latter-day Saints. It did not look like the building in my dreams, but I wanted to find out what was there and if it had any connection with what actually kept coming into my dreams all the time. I felt like I was being pushed to the church in Kwe Kwe. So I went to that church on Sunday. The meeting had started when I arrived. It was actually not easy for me to walk in there.

I was at the back. It was a fast Sunday. I didn't know what was going on. People got up to give testimonies. I didn't know what they were doing. Yet I felt like I was among good friends. So I got up and went straight to the pulpit and started talking. I was shaking. My heart was beating very fast. It was not easy for me to talk to people I didn't know. I asked them to forgive me if I made any mistake. I stood in front of these people to talk about my feelings. I felt that I was with people I knew a long time ago. I never felt like I was a stranger there. I don't know how to express that feeling. I said that I believed in a supreme being called God, and I wanted to be a member of his church.

I finished and had just started to walk back when they all responded with a big "Amen." That was the welcome I had. I then took a place beside Sister Hamstead, the wife of the mission president. After the meeting she told me about the plan of salvation and showed me a picture of the Salt Lake Temple. I was very excited to see that picture, for it was the same building that I had seen in my dreams. The feeling that actually descended upon the two of us, I cannot explain. Before I came away I was weeping. I can't explain the feeling. I was released of all burdens. I felt I had gone to a place where I had visited often, and now I was at home. I felt that this was the true Church and that I should join it.

I was given a copy of the Book of Mormon by Sister Hamstead the very day I went to church in Kwe Kwe. I never put it down. I read it through. Nobody can tell me that book is not true. Everybody should read it.

I received the lessons, and it went very fast—maybe because I wanted to know more, or maybe because I was an easy student. It took about a week or two to prepare me for baptism. When I had finished with the lessons, I realized that I really might have met those people who were attending church in Kwe Kwe sometime long ago. I knew that we were a family.

I now have devoted my own day of fasting and prayer to the Almighty. I devote every Tuesday to fasting and praying. To be honest, I'm happy. I'm very happy.

I believe Joseph Smith's testimony because of what I saw in my dreams. Joseph Smith was actually telling us the truth. He saw exactly what he said he saw, the Father and the Son.

I am prepared to stand in front of the world and say that I have found the true Church. Our Father presides over all things. The Church of Jesus Christ of Latter-day Saints is the only true church.

The greatest change that has come into my life because of the gospel has been the realization that we are actually on earth as a big family. Most of us just don't know ourselves and our relationship with our fellowmen. Coming to know this was a very big change in my life. We will truly get to know ourselves when Jesus Christ returns to earth to take his people with him. Let's live in peace. Let's pray for peace.

14

Ernest Sibanda

I Am a Free Man

Ernest Sibanda was the first black to join the Church in Zimbabwe. He was born in Harare, Zimbabwe, on 25 December 1925. After completing his elementary and high schooling, he studied at the university for seven years, completing B.A. and B.S. degrees. He served as a Seventh Day Adventist pastor for three years, as a teacher for nine years, and as a headmaster for fifteen years. He and his wife, Priscilla, whom he married in 1958, are the parents of three children. Through the tragedy of war, which left Brother and Sister Sibanda destitute, they came in contact with the Church when missionaries gave them a copy of the Book of Mormon. They were baptized in January 1979 and endured painful challenges as the first blacks to enter a white branch in Zimbabwe.

I started herding cattle when I was about four years old. This was in 1930. In the morning I went to school, and in the afternoon I went to herd cattle, until it was time to take them back home to the corral. It is a traditional law that a boy is for herding cattle and a girl is for washing and cooking at home. According to African ways, no matter how old you are, if some of your relatives are still alive, you have to abide by this law. Even now, when I am an old man, because I am still called someone's son, brothers to my father can still have me go and look after cattle—it's still traditional law. If I don't do it, they'll start thinking that I'm very unruly, that I don't listen to parents, and so on.

When I was young, we used to have bad experiences herding cattle. If it rained, you didn't rush home. You remained with the cattle. There used to be wild beasts. They could kill a goat, a cow, a sheep. If you lose a goat, parents want to know where you have been. You may get some caning for being careless with property.

Once, when I was driving cattle home, there was a big snake along the way. I could see cattle running away, but I wanted to see the snake. I didn't know it was a big python. The python wanted to swallow one of the goats. I had to fight the python, and it wanted to bring its tail round to me. I had to leave the cattle and rush home to tell my father. My father brought a spear with him, and he had to kill the python. The python had the goat right inside its tummy; it came up in a great heap, and it couldn't move. When they skinned the python, the whole goat came out as it was, but it was already dead. Some people took the goat and ate it. I was surprised they ate it, because this goat was not killed by man but by a reptile.

Another experience we had was with a leopard, a very cunning animal. A leopard went to run off with a calf, and got up into a tree with it. None of us could go and throw stones, so there came a big boy, older than me. He got a stone to throw. Then the leopard jumped on him, got on the back of his head, and took the whole skin that covered his face. He didn't die. People took him, took some leaves from trees, and made a medicine that brought the skin back. The skin went all right, but the boy was never normal. When he went to school, others laughed. He was never married. Yes, we met many experiences when we were herding cattle. We used to walk without shirts, just with pants, and we wore no shoes. We were given a spear as protection. That was the greatest weapon at that time. A man without a spear was too ashamed to speak to another man.

I went to school as well. I studied to be a teacher, and I got a Bachelor of Arts degree, and then began studying for a Bachelor of Science. After these studies, I stayed on at the college to be taught to be a pastor. My father was a pastor for the Seventh Day Adventist church. I grew up in this church and believed it was the right church. I was in that church for many years, from boyhood up to manhood. When I became a pastor, I went to replace my father—I had to take the very same church where he had been. I was a pastor, until I couldn't take it anymore. When I say I couldn't take it anymore, I am not talking against the Lord. I am talking against the man-made ways—the ways that were made by some pastors, who taught that whosoever is not a Seventh Day Adventist member will never see the kingdom of heaven. This made me a bit cross, because everybody was created by the Lord. I didn't like it anymore, so I became a headmaster, and was controlling a school.

When I met my wife, we were both working in schools. We could think of nothing but one another. We waited three years before we got married, but we were already in love. So we both announced such news to our parents. The *lobola* was paid. This means dowry. Some head of cattle were driven from my home to my father-in-law. This is a great law among Africans. If you don't pay *lobola*, in-laws never regard you as their son, only as a friend of their daughter. We had a feast to allow my relatives and friends to meet at the in-laws' home. We married in 1958.

It took us about four years to have a child. We did not want many. We wanted one or two, but the Lord did not agree with us. He gave us the number that he wanted.

Then war started, and we had a very hard time. We were living in a new home, belonging just to me and my wife, on the outskirts of Harare. One night was a terrible night. On 11 April 1976 our home was bound by terrorist forces, who came to me and my wife when it was about nine o'clock at night. They had guns with them, and they asked us to come out of the house. When we came out of the house, they ordered us to sit down, to squat on the ground. No movement was supposed to be done by us. They did this because they believed that we were selling them to the white people—they termed us as "sell-outs." They shot three bullets, and from those bullets, the house caught fire. It was a grass-thatched house. All the furniture, the carpets and whatnot, got burned. Our children were safe because they were with my parents. The terrorists moved to a cattle crop, where I kept forty-one head of cattle, and they shot them all—they left not even one. It was about midnight when they walked away. My home was the ninth home to be burned—other people had their homes burned before.

This may have been the Lord's plan. I hope so, and I believe in that. All the property we had was burned. I was left in pajamas, and my wife was left in a night dress. We had nothing with us. We slept without food, without blankets, without clothes, and without cleaning ourselves. We didn't have any alternative but to run away. We couldn't walk to Harare, because of the war—we were trying to be away from the areas where we had seen disaster. So we began walking a journey of 150 miles, towards Bulawayo. We were not properly dressed, so we thought it was much better to walk by night, and through the field, not by the highway. We would remain in hiding for the whole day, up till about ten o'clock in the night, and then we could start. I could walk faster than my wife, and we always had to sit down and have a rest. When we finally got to a stream, we were both very thirsty, but the stream was very dirty.

We needed some water to drink, so we chose to drink it. Today, I couldn't drink it.

When we had walked about 150 miles, we found a very kind man, who said we could sit at the back of his truck, where his pigs were. We were quite happy to have a lift. When we came into Bulawayo, another kind man gave us a lift to his house—he was a white man of the Roman Catholic church. Then we were safe. We had food. We had some clothes. We cleaned ourselves, and for a month we were just sitting by the man's house—he was a very, very kind man.

From there on, we stayed in Bulawayo. We were offered some jobs to do. My first job was for about ten dollars a month. My wife had a very poor job, where she could earn very little money. Then in 1979 I worked for a different man, who paid me fifteen dollars a month.

In December 1979 two young men came on bicycles to where I worked, and pressed the bell. My employer came out. He knew these young people who wore such very clean, well-shaven hair, white shirts, and different trousers, but who were on bicycles. Then my employer pointed his finger at me, and I came closer to him. He said, "This young man wants to talk to you." One of the young men said they were from a church named The Church of Jesus Christ of Latter-day Saints. I had not known of such an organization when I grew up. When Elder Kaelin and Elder Black talked, I listened very carefully. When they showed me the Book of Mormon, I wanted to know what sort of a book it was. I asked if they could lend it to me, and they agreed.

I went through a few pages, and the following morning they came back. I asked them to extend the time that I should read, so I could better understand the book. They agreed with me. The third day, when they came in, I asked them how long it was going to take them to baptize me. They were surprised to hear me ask for baptism. They told me the following: "Before we baptize you, Mr. Sibanda, we are supposed to teach you. It will take us a few weeks to teach you." I wanted to know what they would teach me. I had read the Bible for a long time. I felt I had known the gospel for a long time—and what else could they teach me? Well, they came to teach me exactly what I was never taught before. It was very interesting to me.

The following week, I was baptized. You know, instead of being baptized once, I was in the water three times. The first time, the elder never said "Amen" at the end of the prayer. The second time, my hair was not deep into the water. My grandson began to beat a sister on the shoulder when he saw me getting baptized—he thought I was drowned. The third time, I was baptized properly. The whole congregation was happy, looking at me with such smiles. The district president rang Johannesburg, telling the mission president that they had baptized an African. I was the first African to be baptized in Rhodesia [now Zimbabwe]. There was joy.

When I was baptized, I felt very free. I felt released from every evil. I found there was love in me for my family. I found there was love within me for the Church. I felt, to sum up, very free. I am a free man.

Within a few weeks, my wife was baptized. Three to four weeks following, my two daughters were baptized. Then my son was baptized. To make it quite clear, I should say the whole family is a family of Latter-day Saints. One day the mission president from Johannesburg flew to Bulawayo. The first member to be greeted by President LeBaron was my wife. My wife was so happy to shake hands with a man of that position. I was used to members of the Church shaking hands with me.

When I became a member I got many friends, friends who could advise me of the good things on earth. I got many brethren. I got many sisters. I had the Church, when other friends and relatives could not help me.

I was the first black man to join the Church here. When I first joined, I was a little bit disturbed, because some people didn't like an African in the Church. When I was confirmed and introduced to the members of the branch, some never raised their hands to sustain me. When I sat for a Church meeting, some members would tell me to move. They would say, "I've been here for seven years with my children and my wife. Will you please try the other bench?" At last my branch president, President Eppel, gave my family a bench to sit at. One day I stood up to people who were telling me to move. I said, "If anyone brought furniture from home into the chapel, please take it back. Leave what belongs to the Church. I'll never move." That was the end of that story.

Once I stood to give a lesson in a classroom. Some questioned, "Who is he to teach us? A black man, teaching us?" Then I stood firm. I said, "Brethren, if we are all Latter-day Saints, and I am assigned by the Lord to teach, then I have to teach you." The members had to sit and listen to me, though some had funny expressions on their faces. But the Lord gave them the message.

Combining two races is not easy. With all of these problems, I did not leave. The Church doesn't belong to a human being. The

Church belongs to the Lord. The Lord never gave me problems — he loved me coming back to his church. Therefore, I wouldn't leave. I came to worship. These problems from some of the other members continued, though they now are fading off. Some problems, like people asking new black members to move away, are no more. We have a good number of black people attending the branch. I used to count up to fifty. They like coming in.

Within a few weeks after my baptism, I was made a young people's Sunday School president. When I was released, I was made a branch clerk. After that, I received a calling as second counselor in the branch presidency.

In 1985 I felt sick. For about one year, I was lying in the hospital. My wife and children were left at home. I had a clot of blood in my back, so blood couldn't circulate in the veins. Nobody thought I was going to walk again, but prayers were made by the elders. They would come and see me in the hospital. Then I became better.

A few weeks after leaving the hospital, I lost my daughter, on 28 February 1986. She got burned in her car, together with her husband. They had gallons of gas in the car, and they got in a head-on collision, and all the gallons opened and spilt on them. The whole car got burned, including the engine and gas tank. This is the information I got from the police.

When we collected the news that my daughter had died, we rang the branch president. Immediately, he came to my house. He left one hundred dollars with us that we could use on expenses of the funeral. So we had very good help from the Church. The funeral was very beautiful, though it was sorrowful to us. I know my daughter is having a rest now.

When we thought that we were coming to the end of troubles, our house was burglarized, in 1987. When my wife and children were at church, the burglars pulled out our refrigerator, a deep freezer, a stove, plus little items like clothing and salt. We were left again with very little to wear. When this happened, I thought of the missionaries, who used to help me before they went away. I wrote a letter to an elder in Utah. A good number of clothes were donated and sent to us. What a wonderful help! We are still dressing in the clothes they donated to us. This showed us a spirit of unity.

These are some of the misfortunes I have come across. However, they did not bring so much problem to me, because the Saints came to our aid. They helped us. This has pulled me a long way, helping me know that I should remain within the Church for the rest of my life.

I have been given an assignment of translating hymns from English to Shona. This assignment was given to me by the mission president. I'm still doing it. It's going to take me a little bit of time to finish, because some of the hymns require a very careful concentration. There are some words in English that we haven't got in my own language. But I'll try to fit it. One difficult thing is that we don't read music. We sing from our heads. As long as you tell us the hymn number, so we can read the words, we can sing.

I did my genealogy. My grandfather was a pioneer. He saw white people first come to Rhodesia [now Zimbabwe]. He was a messenger, and would walk nearly two hundred miles with one letter. He saw Cecil Rhodes and David Livingstone. He even pioneered going to Victoria Falls, when this wonderful place was found. He told me there were a lot of mosquitoes and a lot of flies, and many people died. Because of the jungles, nobody had gone to Victoria Falls before then. Not many people wanted to go to the place, because it was dangerous. But he was there.

I am sure my parents are waiting for me to do their temple work. They were good Christians. I've often told my children that if I loved my wife as my father loved his, I would be a great man. My father never allowed my mother to work hard. He could not eat before my mother had taken food. He always said his wife was someone very beautiful. She was an honorable mother, and she loved the whole family. They were not in the true Church, because they died before the Church was introduced to them. If they were alive today, they would have joined the Church with me. So they are waiting for me to help them. I'll soon go to Johannesburg, to the temple, to stand for them and do the work, that they might have the opportunity to receive the blessings of the gospel. And, of course, I also can do the work for my daughter and her husband, in regard to their sealing.

I had an experience that didn't bring happiness to me. We were preparing to go and see the temple in Johannesburg. We thought that we could simply walk in and see the temple. We knew that we had to dress in white, but we did not know of other requirements. Two days before we went off, I was given a dream. In the dream, someone was speaking to me, someone who was very special, tall, and very clean, without any marks on him. Then a voice came to me and said, "My house is very clean. I do not allow any marks in it." Then I awoke and got up in the night. I said to my wife, "Priscilla, I'm surprised I'm having this dream." My wife asked me, "What evil did you do?" I said, "My dear, I have never done any evil." She said, "But why this dream? You go to bed. Maybe you'll get the same dream again." I went back to bed. I was in tears. Then I could see someone wiping off tears from my face. The person wasn't wiping with a handkerchief, but was using a finger. That finger was very soft, as soft as cotton. I woke and couldn't sleep again. All night I was up. I started reading and singing to myself, just to drive away this dream. But I couldn't drive it away. I remained thinking of it until we went off.

When we got to Johannesburg, I was told I should have a temple recommend from my branch president. I was surprised. I had come from Zimbabwe and hadn't carried a temple recommend with me. I didn't blame them for demanding this. I knew the Lord had spoken to me in my dream. I should have thought of this and rushed to the branch president. We came back without seeing the temple. We could see its beauty, but we didn't go in. But we have saved our money again, and we will go to the temple, when the weather is a little bit warmer.

As old as I am, it's not easy to look back. It's only easy to look forward. There is life where I am headed. There is death on the earth. Those who accept this gospel will feel themselves free. Life is life after receiving the word of God. Without the word of the Lord, you are a man in different walks. The Lord speaks. He has never been silent since he created man. He speaks. He has spoken to me many times.

15

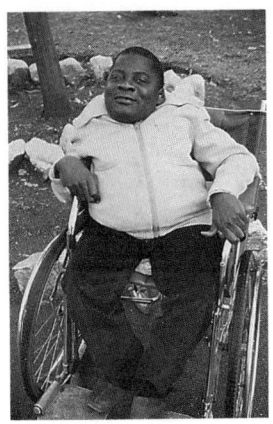

Sabbath Sibanda Maturure

Only God Knows Our Problems

Sabbath Sibanda Maturure was born on 28 December 1952 in Shurugwi, Zimbabwe, to a family of eleven children of the Shona tribe. He and three of his sisters were born with a debilitating disease which confined him to a wheelchair and took the life of two of his sisters. The effects of this disease and the unexpected death of his mother caused Sabbath to struggle with self-pity and bitterness. Through coming to learn of God's love for him and developing faith in Christ, Sabbath began to live a happy and fulfilled life of service. He married his wife, Susan, in 1975, and they are the parents of three daughters. In August 1986 Sabbath joined the Church and has served as a Sunday School teacher in the Bulawayo Branch.

I was born in Shurugwi, Zimbabwe, on 28 December 1952 into a family of eleven—seven girls and four boys. Four of us were born disabled: two older sisters, me, and a younger sister. Our bodies were shrunken, our legs were deformed, and our hands were weak. I didn't understand why I couldn't play with the other children.

It was so fortunate that my father was brought up in a Christian family. The farm on which we were living belonged to the Methodists. We were all born there. My two older sisters have since died.

My mother used to carry me on her back, and when she would go to the fields, when things were green, she would carry us one by one on her back. She would take us to see what was happening in the fields. She didn't show any preference for any of her children over the others.

When I was brought to the Jairos Jiri Handicap Center, I was the youngest one there. I cried all day long. The only person whom I loved was my mother. I didn't have anyone else to think of. So the only person who I thought was going to look after me was my mother. I was eight years of age when I was separated from her. It was a terrible blow. I really missed my mother. I even hated the minister who brought me up here. I thought he was very cruel to us.

I was born in an African hut, grass thatched and not very tall in structure. When I came up here the buildings were very tall, and they were rather clean. I really felt out of place. The idea of my mother going away was really a blow.

A year later, in 1962, I met a talented young friend who was disabled in the same way I was. His name was Samuel Parlor. He introduced me to art. We used to draw and paint together. We used to discuss our life histories. Samuel has a sister who also is disabled. We used to criticize God for having created us this way. We used to wonder as to why he should create us in this manner. So there was nothing good about God that we knew of.

My sisters used to ask me to go to church, because we were brought up by the reverend who was a Methodist minister. I didn't really want to go to church. The more Samuel and I drew, the more critical we became. We even became critical of the administration of the Jairos [handicap] association. We didn't really know why they should worry about educating us.

Samuel, who was now my best friend, and I used to go to the trade fair. Since we were talented in art, we used to be taken to the trade fair so that people could admire our work and see what the Jairos association was doing for all of us. Since we had no allowance from our parents, people used to give us some small tokens of money. We would keep this money for our pocket money. We would buy whatever we wanted: pens, paints, and whatever.

Samuel became very close to me. We used to ride together on the same wheelchair. We used to buy clothes that were the same, and then people thought we were twins. He was second only to my mother.

In December 1969 Samuel went home. I also went to my home in Shurugwi. When I came back Samuel was not well. All that year he was kept in bed. He had some breathing problems, and since his body was not strong enough, it couldn't hold up anymore. So he died. It was the hardest thing for me during that time. The center of my life was again empty.

I lived on the hope that I would see my mother, because she was the only person that I thought of now. In December 1970 somebody was kind enough to drive me and my sister home on Christmas Day. When we got there we realized that our mother was sick too. Three hours later our mother died.

It all became dark. I couldn't even feel the pain during that time. My mind stopped thinking, and I couldn't even feel the impact of that pain. It took a long time for me to realize that my mother had actually died.

On the following day, other people came to me, and there was a minister there. People were crying. They were saying, "What is going to happen to these disabled people? Who is going to look after them after the death of their mother?" They were so worried, but this Methodist minister said to them, "Please keep quiet. The Lord is going to look after them." I don't know why I really took these words in, but I still remember them.

So my mother was buried, and there was nothing left for me. Life was hopeless then. Then I came up again to the handicap center.

I didn't know then the glory that is behind God. Now I'm shedding tears of joy because I know that my mother lives, and I know that if my mother had not lived in the Lord, she wouldn't have looked after us. With the present life that I'm leading, I know that I'm going to meet my mother in a time of glory.

I used to go to the trade fair to draw and paint. We were in one of the big halls where we had our Jairos Jiri stand. A stand in front of us was artistically painted, and I admired it. I used to see a lot of young people, both black and white, coming in and going out. On this stand were big words written in red, "God loves you." I used to ask myself this question: "How, how could God love people? Does he love me? Does he love those people who are going in there?" There was no one who would come up and talk to me. I wanted to meet someone from there. But I had no courage to go there and ask. On a certain day, a girl named Wendy came up to our stand. She looked at my work. She admired my work, and she spent quite some time standing there. I asked her if I could help her. She was very kind. I could see that she was sincere in whatever she was asking.

She said, "I am just seeing what you are doing." Then she asked me my name, and I told her. She said, "Your name is Sabbath?" I said, "Yes. Sabbath." "Do you know what it means?" she asked. I said, "Yes. My mother told me that it means 'the day of prayer.' " But she then said to me, "You know, Sabbath, I happen to come from South Africa, and we have come here to talk to the people about God. You see over at that stand, 'God loves you.' " I said, "I heard that people are saying that God loves all of us. But does he love me as well?" My question didn't disappoint her, and the way she answered really encouraged me to ask more. She said, "Yes. God loves you. This is why you are here." I said, "But you are different. Look, you are smart, you are smartly dressed. You can walk and what have you." Then she said to me, "But, Sabbath, you can paint. I can't." She went on talking to me and convinced me that God loved me. She got some pamphlets for me. I brought them to the center. During that evening one of our friends was sick, so the lights were on. It took quite some time for us to get to sleep, so I turned to those pamphlets and read them.

Afterwards I had this desire in me to know more about God. I went to a friend and asked for a Bible. He was surprised to hear my request. But then I took the Bible and read it. And then I went to church. And the first sermon that I heard was on the tenth chapter of John. This man was preaching about Christ, who has his sheep, and the sheep hear his voice. I asked myself as to whether I was one of the flock. The answer came to me that I was one of the Lord's sheep, and I should hear God's voice. I accepted Jesus Christ. Since that time I have put all my problems to Christ. I used to wonder why I was being educated and why I was living. All those doubts went away. I began to love everybody. I began to share my problems with other people. I began to have a new life. I began to go to church. I began to share the word of God with other people that came to me.

When Wendy went away we wrote to each other. She sent me a collapsible wheelchair. It became easier for me to go anywhere to share the word of God. Then I got married.

I met my wife through my sister who was disabled and was living at the center. They used to go to church together. I didn't fall in love with her before I became a Christian. We got married because she was the only person who understood my sister's problems. We got quite close because we used to go to church together. My wife is also disabled. Her left leg is in a brace. She works in town, where she met Elder Lake, who brought us the Church.

I paid my *lobola* of seven head of cattle, and $280 in the form of cash. I used to sell my paintings to make money. My sisters loved my wife very much, and they were very talented in crocheting and knitting. So they used to fund-raise to help me pay the *lobola*.

I got married, and God helped us, although I wasn't generating enough income. People whom we preached to brought us food. They used to help us pay our rent. I was the chairman of the trainees representative council.

Some people face challenges like mine. Some of them are born being able to walk, and then they become disabled. So they have problems. But I'm so glad that I'm able to talk to them and share with them my experience. Now I've got three physically fit daughters.

I can tell you how we came to be members of the Church. My wife, Susan, happened to be working for a Jairos Jiri craft shop somewhere in town, where a lot of tourists come. Susan happened to see a tall white man. He had a name tag which read, "Elder Boyd Lake." When Susan saw him, she smiled at him. Elder Lake came and talked to her. Susan asked Elder Lake what his church was and what it was all about. She invited Elder Lake to come up to our place to meet us. Then I met Elder and Sister Lake. Elder Lake talked to us about Christ and about the priesthood. He had first been baptized in the Methodist church, where they sprinkle the people. Elder Lake talked all about these things. They brought us the Book of Mormon.

Our interest grew, and our friendship grew. One day when the missionaries came, I had a headache. They laid their hands on my head, and they prayed very hard for me. And, to my uttermost surprise, during that evening I was better! It was quite some time before I suffered from headaches again.

So I entertained the idea of joining the Church, but there was a step that we didn't know about yet—learning about the Restoration brought about through Joseph Smith. I said to Elder Lake, "Can I join the Church? Can I be baptized? Can my family be baptized?" Once I learned of Joseph Smith's revelations, we took our time to study the gospel, and I was baptized.

My greatest hope in life is to serve God. I have given myself a duty that I must work for God, tell all my disabled brothers and sisters about God, tell everyone I meet about God. I pray very hard that one day I will be married in the temple. I pray that someday—I have no doubt that one day this will happen—I will be able to do some missionary work to tell more people about God.

When I look at my life, I realize that the most painful thing that a human being can come across is to think that he can do everything on his own. But I've since surrendered everything to Christ. If I've got problems, I just give them to him, and if I don't get what I want, I know that God has not given me that. If I ask for certain things and I don't get them, I know that God doesn't want them that way.

Every day I teach my children. I instruct them and myself that God should direct our everyday work. When my family has the last prayer of the evening, we say, "God, we go to sleep now. Direct us in our daily activities tomorrow." God is right in front. The beginning of wisdom is in God. If people are truly wise, they can only get their wisdom from the word of God.

I have got a very strong belief that the gospel is true. I know that the Church is true. I know that the prophets are true. And I have no doubt that anybody who gives himself to Christ will have eternal life, along with every faithful member of his family. I believe that if every one of us can continue to be better Christians, working harder and harder, we'll all have eternal life.

It is my sincere hope that everyone who listens to my testimony will try to seek for direct communication with God. Only God knows our problems and how to help us with them. If we've got any abilities, and it doesn't matter how small they seem, to God they are important. Give them to him by using them to serve others, as Christ did. My hope is that everyone in my family, and their generations that will follow, will serve Christ.

16

Julia N. Mavimbela

Where There Has Been a Bloodstain, a Beautiful Flower Must Grow

Julia N. Mavimbela has given years of selfless service to her people and to her country. After a career of teaching, she continues to serve in community, national, and international organizations for women's rights and for peace. In spite of tragedies in her life, Julia refused to allow bitterness or hatred to enter her heart. Her life and service have inspired many others. Born on 20 December 1917 in Standerton, South Africa, Julia married John Mavimbela in 1946. They had seven children. In 1981 Julia accepted the gospel and threw her energies into missionary work and Church service. She has served as Relief Society president and was the special guest speaker at the BYU Women's Conference of 1989.

I was born in 1917, just as World War I was coming to an end, to a very humble family of one brother and four sisters. My father loved music and formed my family into a choir. Though I was young, I was always wanting to know how he was performing and conducting. I remember one time at church he actually had to give me a little hiding because I was disturbing him when he was conducting the choir.

My father died when I was only four years old, going on five. I lived with my mother in town in order to get a better education. My mother struggled to make a living as a washerwoman. She had a special way of ironing standard collars for ministers and members of dance groups. I told her not to worry. I would go and teach on a farm school. I lived among the farm people and learned to do with them whatever work they did. I learned to drive mules, and I can drive a span of six.

My college experience was very exciting, because I became chief monitor. I had to take care of three hundred girls in the absence of the matron.

When I completed school, I applied for a teaching post in different schools and with different religious denominations. The Methodists liked me and gave me a school in Springs, Transvaal.

I qualified as a teacher in all subjects in all age groups. I got my provincial certificate, which qualified me to teach in any school. And I loved children.

I later took two years of special methods courses in teaching kindergarten. While teaching kindergarten, I had a breakthrough: I was the first woman to be granted a principalship. I had twenty teachers under my care at a school in Boxburg.

Although I think young men were always looking at me, it wasn't easy for me to decide to get married, because I was very concerned about my mother. The first men who wanted to have my hand in marriage couldn't win me. Among those offering was a Methodist minister, but I pushed him away. I just thought I was not meant for marriage. I was aware that if I got married, my husband might tell me to have nothing to do with my mother, and she was very special to me.

Then my mother's health failed, and she died suddenly. I was sad, because I had looked forward to my mother being with me to help me make a decision about marriage.

I heard of a gentleman who had been having eyes for me, and because I was now older in my years, my heart decided he was the right man. He would understand me. "Okay, I can get married," I said. He had to go to my brother and pay dowry. I still have the receipt: 120 pounds, which is 240 rand today.

We got married in the Methodist church, and I won't forget it. My husband-to-be forgot the ring, but he wanted the ceremony to go through. So he excused himself and bought a curtain ring at the nearest shop, and that was it. The real ring that I received later was a beautiful golden ring. I was quite happy.

Both of us felt that if we could work together, there would be progress. So I gave up my teaching and went to help my husband run a little butcher and grocery shop he had in Eastern Native

Township. My husband and my future were more important to me than my teaching.

My husband was a very special man. I had a salary, and the money was my own. I banked it and never told him, and he never wanted to know where it had gone or what I had done with it.

He was also community oriented. When I was with my friends, he would go to the kitchen and wash up the dishes. When there was a baby, he would help me wash the napkins [diapers]. I had five girls and one boy.

On 9 June 1955 my husband died tragically. As the founder of the Black-African Chamber of Commerce in Johannesburg, one day he was planning a big meeting. He left in the morning. I was spring-cleaning the house, with the aid of another young lady, when suddenly at about seven in the evening somebody came to the door. "Is your husband home?" he asked.

"No, he is about to arrive."

He was asking that question because he had already heard that a car that fit the description of my husband's was wrecked on the roadside.

When we got to the scene of the accident, I saw that it was my husband's car. I collapsed. He had already died. It was a head-on collision.

The next day a black policeman came to the house and asked me to go to the police station. "I have never seen so much money on a man," he said. I knew that with his business my husband had to carry a lot of money, to pay for the livestock he bought. The farmers did not take checks, only cash.

We went to the police station, where I demanded anything the police had collected from the car. Believe it or not, I got only seven pounds and nineteen cents.

I shook my head. "This can't be right. He must have had hundreds, for I know what he had to do."

"That is it. There is nothing more," they told me.

So I went home and buried my husband. I heard that the previous day the police had told a minister of the Methodist church that "a rich kaffir is dead." The minister came to comfort me, but I told him, "No, Reverend, it is over. Let's look for tomorrow."

It was quite clear that the other man involved in the accident was on my husband's side of the road. He was white. Most of the policemen were white. The police said, "The careless drivers are the blacks."

I was two months expectant. I carried the baby and ran my husband's business under that strain.

All this went to make me become a very bitter woman. I forgave the man who caused the accident, for I knew that accidents were inevitable. But the lawyer and the laws of the country had passed their judgment because of color.

One day when we were at my church, reading the scriptures on the crucifixion of our Lord Jesus Christ, I was touched by what the Lord said: "Forgive them; for they know not what they do" (Luke 23:34). I was really, really touched by that. This was the beginning of my feeling that I should never throw a stone at other people, and that I should forgive others. I told myself there must be a change in my life. But I was not yet in the church that could really make me forgive. The people around me in my church just made my hatred grow bigger and bigger.

Some of my church friends volunteered to assist me in my community projects, and they sent me a little token of 150 rand, donated by a group in America, every three months. I used the money in my projects, like gardening and youth clubs. But I used to never get that 150 rand regularly; the pastor would take it and pocket it, believe it or not! I didn't take exception, though. I told myself, "I will work very hard as long as I live, because I find joy in it. I am not doing it for men. I am doing it for the glory of my God." I wrote to the people in America and told them, "Don't ever send the money again. The Lord has shown me something." By then, I no longer belonged to that church.

I was trying at this time to find an answer to my bitterness. I met a group of men and women who had an ideology of absolute honesty, absolute love, absolute unselfishness, and absolute purity. These people had a great influence on me, but I couldn't keep up with their progress because they were traveling abroad extensively. I was with my little children and felt I could not afford to get away, for they were very young when my husband died. So I was beginning to work with other people, selected people, while others I hated.

Then, in 1976 we had the racial riots in Soweto. These could have opened up the same wound again in my life. I looked at the younger people, and they had their side of life, their way of thinking, their bitterness—which they expressed openly. They didn't want to even *see* a white; and I thought that maybe the Lord could use me to help them, because I knew what it was like to feel isolated because of one's own confusion. So I started a project in Soweto to bring young people into doing things, trying to help them find a message in what they did.

I was doing community service during the worst of the riots in Soweto. As I moved around, I tried to convince the youth to do something for themselves other than to feel dejected. I used to call them up and say a few words.

When I was involved in a planting project with them, I would say, "Now look, boys and girls, as we see this soil down here, it is solid and hard; but if we push a spade or a fork down into it, we will crack it and come out with lumps of dirt. And then if we break those lumps and throw in a seed, the seed will grow. This is my message to you young people. You should have it in your hearts. Let us dig into the soil of bitterness, throw in a seed, show love, and see what fruits it can give. Love will not come without forgiving others. Where there has been a bloodstain, a beautiful flower must grow."

I wouldn't tell the young people my personal story, but I knew that deep in my heart I had been touched by Jesus' words: "Forgive them; for they know not what they do."

I think I could say that I was very successful. The whole idea of forgiving spread very gradually but surely.

When I was visited by another organization, bigger than mine, which came to ask me to clean out a boys' club, I said to them, "How is it that out of the many, many women you see in Soweto, you have chosen me to do this Cinderella work?" They couldn't answer. I said, "Girls, look, you've really always had the upper hand among other willing people. You get the reins. I get the slavery. I am not prepared to do this project."

They went away, and I just said, "Why, out of so many people, did they ask me? Well, let me humble myself."

The following day, when I arrived at the boys' club, I saw two young men, in work clothes, dust on top of them, in the heat. I said to myself, "How can there be boys here, white boys for that matter?"

I walked through the gate. They said, "Hi."

"How are you?" I replied.

"We're all right."

"What are you doing here?"

"We're cleaning."

"Cleaning? Where do you come from?"

"From America."

"America? How did you come to clean in Soweto?"

"We read in the paper the advertisement about the boys' club."

I said, "Okay," and walked into the office. I had hardly been seated, when I heard footsteps.

"We have come to greet you. We want to shake your hand and tell you that since we have been working here"—they said it had been three weeks or three months, I can't remember which—"we have never had a warmer handshake, and we feel this greeting was special."

Next they asked, "Can we visit your home?"

I looked at these young men. "Visit my home? No." Any home that has a white visitor is called a "sell-out."

Then I relented and said, "All right, I'll think about it and tell you later."

They left the office.

They continued to work, and I made a decision to come and help them clean up. My honor was not my worry. I would just do what I felt was good for the black boys who played in the center.

Finally I told the young men, "Give me a chance to go clean up my house. You must not look at my face and think that my house is as my face. Cobwebs hang in my house. So three days from today, I will clean up, and you can visit me."

At the set date and time, the two young men came, all dressed up. They called themselves "elders." "Oh, no," I said to myself. "I should be in another place. Elders are something very special in churches. How can they visit the home of an ordinary woman like me?"

They came, took seats, said a prayer with me, and explained who they were. Then they started the first lesson—which carried no weight with me. "I can't be moving from one church corner to another," I told them.

They made another appointment and left. What was strange to me is that I just felt they should come, so I let them continue to come.

On the second visit, they saw a wonderful picture of my wedding, and they asked, "Where is he?"

"Oh, he has passed on."

"Do you know that you can be baptized for him?"

Something opened in my mind. "Take baptism for him? In what way?"

They explained how.

I said to them, "Look here, Elders"—I had started addressing them as Elders—"you have startled me. I am a black, and in other churches when you speak about the dead, you get excommunicated. Now you come and tell me about my dead. You've got a different message. Come again."

So they returned, and I started to listen to them. I remember the first question I asked: "Do you in your church repeat the Apostles' Creed?"

"No."

As a child in my church, I had never repeated the creed because I did not understand it. I would be quiet when in the Methodist church people said, "I believe in the holy catholic church."

That was the beginning of a great new day in my life. I started to see that I had real, true brothers in my home.

One day I said to them, "Come along. We'll have supper together." I had just a little last bit of money, so I was able to get to town and buy what I thought would be to their delight.

On the way home from town, I sat next to another woman in the taxi, and I was so interested in my visit from the missionaries that I started to talk about what I had heard. She listened with interest as the taxi moved toward Soweto.

When we parted at my destination, I picked up my bag but left my groceries. When it came to me that my groceries were not with me, the taxi was gone; and the missionaries were on their way, and I had promised them dinner. "What will I do?" I thought.

I said, "Lord, if I could give these groceries to someone who is more in need than me, I am satisfied. It is okay."

When I got home, I realized I had no candle; the candles were in with my groceries. Then a car stopped, and out came the missionaries. I welcomed them in. I said, "Well, Elders, I've been heavily challenged. All that was to make us happy today is gone with the taxi."

Well, missionaries are missionaries. They were very understanding and said it was all right. That was it. We had our lesson.

That was Tuesday. On Wednesday, I decided to go down to see my daughter, to tell her there was not a grain in the house. She works at the Carlton Hotel. I stood beckoning taxis, but none would stop. They just kept on passing. Suddenly, a taxi, when it had gone a few yards away from me, stopped, and out came a woman who beckoned to me and pointed. I ran up to her, got into the taxi, and we drove off.

She addressed me. "Are you the woman I was traveling with yesterday who left your groceries in the car? I've got them."

I could not believe my ears. "Is that why you stopped the taxi?" I asked her.

"Yes," she said. "I recognized you. I'll bring your groceries to your house."

We traveled on. I kept asking her, "Are you serious?"

"Yes," she said.

The next day, she really did come to my home and said, "My children have taken three bananas out of your groceries."

All this happened in the big complex of Soweto, where there were well over a million people.

I saw the beginning of things: When you share with other people, God prepares something in them. The honesty of that woman taught me a lesson.

I was especially grateful for the moment when I met the missionaries, and for what they imparted to me. Out of it came a feeling of forgiveness that would eventually lead to my decision to be baptized. Reading the Book of Mormon changed my whole life. I started to realize that we are but one family.

After I had the lessons from the missionaries, after a couple of months, I felt something that said, "This is the Church." I made the decision to be baptized on 28 November 1981.

I remember the missionaries coming and saying, "Julia, we are going to baptize you on the twenty-eighth of November."

"But why, Elders?"

I think they were testing me to see how decided I was. When the time drew near, I kept on reading the book *Gospel Principles*. I started feeling smaller, doubting myself, whether I was worthy to be baptized. I think I lost several pounds. I was scared. The day came, I went and got baptized.

I wasn't aware that my decision was linked with something unknown to me. When I later got knowledge of my parents, I found that that very day, the twenty-eighth of November, was the day my father had passed away. So that date has meant much to my life.

There was going to be a conference in December of that year, and I was asked to give a talk in Springs. I couldn't believe that President Van Zyl would ask me to give a talk. I felt I had nothing to prepare. But he said, "Just talk."

I never told anybody that I was going to give a talk. All the members of the branch were shocked when they saw me step onto the platform.

The Lord told me just to tell my people how I had felt when my husband tragically died, and how the laws of my country wouldn't satisfy me with the truth, because of my color, but how I had since found myself moving to a very happy state of life. The story about my groceries was the first example. I have also been happier with my neighbors, and have never felt one bit of fear.

A picture of President Spencer W. Kimball hangs in my house. From a glance he looks like P. W. Botha, South Africa's white prime minister. Sometimes people would be angry and ask why I have this white prime minister's picture in my house. When groups come into my house, I stand proud. I tell them without fear who he is, and that they should learn about him someday.

I have felt that the more one gets involved with others, the more one can learn from them. I became very interested in working with women's groups. In 1976 we saw that women of all races needed to unite. We felt concern about our future generations—black, white, yellow, or green; our children would not communicate if we as mothers didn't share our problems and plan a better country for them. We started an organization called Women for Peace. I am amongst the founding members.

We have gone to many authorities and asked for better conditions, for both black and white children. Peace cannot be found when women or other people cannot be fruitfully engaged to better their lives. I also belong to the National Council of Women in South Africa, a multi-racial group that takes interest in the environment of the country—planting trees, improving streets, keeping a strong eye on some of the things relevant to the needs of the blacks.

There is much waste in our country; so we initiated a "Waste Not, Want Not" group.

I have also taught our people about commonsense cures. Families can have a good garden and learn a little bit about canning some of the vegetables or dehydrating them.

Helping others become literate is a work I love. I took special courses in literacy, learning that illiteracy is a barrier. I helped the Zionists group, who elected me as their secretary. I've been serving them for eleven years, and their 783 branches have moved into all corners of the republic. We teach women who cannot read or write.

I love to work with people, but I am a slow-goer with some women in these organizations. I have found that some organizations, instead of building people up, can at times make them feel they are not of worth.

I have traveled extensively in Soweto, knocking at doors with the missionaries, and never for one day have we had opposition. I am convinced that the time is right for the Church in my country. Only our fears may be keeping us from success. The devil has put a spell of uncertainty over Soweto to impede the gospel from progressing. Not only should the families in our branch be satisfied by being part of the Church, but also we should be doing more missionary work. We should invite others into our homes, to share the gospel with them. We should feel that nothing can shake us; what we stand for is the truth. We only need to know what the Holy Ghost wants us to do in these things.

Of course we have had a lot of baptisms in our area. I told myself that as soon as we got to the count of two hundred, I would withdraw from being a missionary and pass it on to others. Then came the riots in Soweto, and the missionaries could no longer come in. I had to accept this situation and realize that their safety should be very important to us.

One day, shortly after our branch had come into Soweto, I went to a leadership meeting. Walking from home, I had to go through a short tunnel. In my heart I was singing "Amazing Grace." Before I knew it, a man grabbed me. I remained cool. I said, "Can I help you? I hope you are aware that I am late. I am going to a church meeting. Can I help you?"

He looked at me, and I could feel his hands loosening from me. I walked out.

As I walked, I heard a voice saying, "Do you know him?"

I answered, "If I had known him, he would be keeping me company."

The voice said, "This world is full of bad people." I continued walking.

One day a group of radicals came to our township. We had suggested in Relief Society that we have a fast for the whole Church, and for the peace of our township. These young radicals could have done the things that they usually did, to any of us, but they peacefully left us.

As Relief Society president to my sisters in Soweto, I have seen that the need here is to help one another in skills and to learn how to conserve food, so that our sisters can make the best of what little they have. For example, we black people have, in the past, invested more in clothes than in anything else. We are trying to help the sisters gradually understand that if they can have just one suit and a good change of clothes and then save more for necessities, they will be better people. We haven't as yet learned the art of saving our money. We need to teach our sisters to save in the common banks, and also to be able to remodel old clothes: Waste not, want not. Small things like proper usage of water have not yet happened. All these things need to be taught to the black sisters.

As I mentioned, the major Church teaching that was a turning point for me was the missionaries' pointing to my husband's picture and saying that I could be baptized for the dead. I said to myself that there could be no better, truer church, for I had always had much love for my parents. I could never understand why I should be taught to forget about them and not be able to mention them. For if I did mention them, I would be excommunicated from my former church. I guess there is fear that people will go back to ancestor worship.

I was also deeply impressed by the first vision of the Prophet Joseph Smith—how he talked directly with God. The scriptural passage James 1:5–6 remains for me a landmark of the changes in my life. I can go directly to God with my concerns. I feel that is a great privilege.

I now approach my children's problems far differently than would a mother who could be pushed and would fight. I have been humbled to know that I should go to my scriptures first, pray over my concern, fast, and then wait to be given a little signal that I can now talk to my children. It is not easy. It has never been easy. I've even felt at times that the answer was taking too long to come. But the more I read of other brothers and sisters in our Church literature, the more I am comforted that everything has got its time, and I must never cease to seek. The challenge I have now is to keep praying and fasting, looking ahead and hoping that my children will also be with me.

When the door opened and I walked into the waters of baptism, I could really feel the cleansing power. I felt real joy.

I also feel I can go into each and every house in my country, and speak to all the people I have been working with in the many organizations I have been part of. I have been able to knock on the doors of big homes in my country. I have ties to important people — ties that pull me toward them. I can't stop my missionary work. That is how I feel.

Going to the temple was like moving from one phase to another. Growing much closer to my maker has made me at times feel that until I do service to others, service of the kind I am receiving, I haven't done enough. I felt when I came into the temple that I belonged. When I used to read before I joined the Church, and I would come to the word *Israel*, I would throw the book aside and say, "It is for the whites. It is not for us. We are not chosen." Today I know I belong to a royal family, if I live righteously. I am an Israelite, and when I was doing my ordinances in the temple, I captured the feeling that we are all on earth as one family.

Being sealed to my husband and my parents was one of the most touching experiences of my life. I could feel my parents next to me. I feel that my parents are grateful that I have done their temple work for them. The Holy Spirit has witnessed this to me.

I wish to tell all my children that this is the true church of our Redeemer and Savior, Jesus Christ. It was no mistake that I made my decision to follow him. I am grateful for the programs of the

Church, and for the leaders, who are inspired by God to pass on to us what the Lord wants us to do.

I am grateful to my parents, who led the way, though they did not know of the gate to becoming Latter-day Saints. I will always be waiting and expecting that we will all be a family forever.

17

Moses Mahlangu

I Waited Fourteen Years

Moses Mahlangu, born on 4 January 1925 in Boshoek, South Africa, to a family of fifteen children, found a Book of Mormon in a library in 1974. As he read it he knew it was true. He had the missionary discussions but was advised to wait to be baptized. For the next sixteen years he distributed copies of the Book of Mormon and other missionary material to his people. Fluent in nine languages, he held regular meetings in his home, where he taught his people from the Book of Mormon. In the spirit of Elias, Brother Mahlangu prepared many of his people for the gospel. He was a true pioneer among the blacks of South Africa. He was baptized in June 1980, and he and his wife, Elizabeth, have three children. He is the elders quorum president in the Soweto Branch and a groundskeeper at the Johannesburg Temple.

I was a very naughty little boy, but when I was about four years old, I did want to know about God. "Where is God?" I asked my father.

"God is in heaven," he told me.

But then I was given strange teachings about God that I could not understand.

My heart was very sore over that. Still, I wanted to understand more, because I heard people talk about God, and when I looked at the flowers and trees and everything, I was told that God had planted all this.

According to our custom, when a young child asks a question, you don't give the right answer. If we asked our mother where her children came from, she might say, "We get them from an airplane," or, "We get them from a river."

I had many sicknesses in my life. When I was about two or three, I became blind. I had a disease, and there were no doctors. When I was about four or five, my eyesight came back again, though one eye still isn't very strong.

After that, there came another sickness which, in our language, we call *winelele*. It is like rheumatism. Early in the morning, my legs and hands were very sore. When I came to Eucliff, the sickness went away, and I didn't have it anymore.

Then came tuberculosis, from age twenty-three to thirty. A leader in my church taught me that I mustn't see a doctor. After a long time, someone said, "If you don't drink our medicine, you must go to stay in the hospital." So I drank it, and in only seven months I was all right. I was treated at home for the next nine years, and then the tuberculosis was gone forever. I wasn't allowed to work during all that time. I sold goods, just trying to stay alive, but not with a license.

My father was a working man. He went to Kimberley, where he joined the Methodist church. When he came to Zebedal, he started a Methodist church there. His brother brought the Lutheran church to Zebedal.

My father was not a minister, only a leader. At school, he only learned to read and to write his name. Then he married my mother. He worked in the mines, then came back home and worked the land. My father and mother had fifteen children. Two of us brothers are still alive.

My father wanted me to go to school, but I didn't want to. I only went for five years. I have learned many languages: English, Afrikaans, Venda, Zonga, Tswana, Ndebe, Xhosa, Swazi, and Zulu. I have learned these languages because I love people. When I have worked with these people, I have asked them, "What is this? What is that?" till I have understood everything. Zulu is closest to my language, because I am Ndebele. Zulu, Ndebele, Swazi, and Xhosa are nearly the same. Tswana, Ndebe, Sotho, and Staping are also nearly the same.

My father also taught me to work. I liked to work, because he showed me how. He was also a hunter and taught me how to hunt animals. I was very excited to bring wild animals in every now and then: the *kudu* [similar to an elk], the *springbok* [similar to an antelope], and a big animal we call a buffalo. Bosso is a land of animals, and the white people liked the skins of jackals, hyenas, tigers, and leopards. That is why I didn't want to go to school; when I woke up, I just wanted to go into the bush and look for wild animals.

My father caught the animals by snaring them, and he also used some strong traps, and some lesser ones. For the dangerous animals, like the leopard, he would dig a pit and put a big trap in it. The animals couldn't get out, and so it was easy to kill them. When my father heard the animals crying out, he would run with the dog to the place and slaughter the animals. Our dogs would run the larger animals until they tired, then we could easily kill them.

Then the white people gave us notice that we musn't kill animals like that anymore. I started to snatch birds, like pigeons and hens, but again, they stopped me from doing that.

My father was a good man; people liked him very much because he helped many people by telling them about the word of God. Because of him, many dangerous people would not fight against one another. When they came to him, he would say, "No, you mustn't fight anybody. When a man fights, he is sick. You must heal him by stopping to talk. When he stops to talk, you heal him."

My father liked to drink, but when he drank, he just slept, and didn't want to wake. The people cried the day he died. During the Boer War, he was on the side of the Boers.

He also knew about herbs to help the body if you had an ailment or a sore. He would give you *mutti*, a leaf which we get naturally from the wild. You cook it and then drink the juice and are healed. Witch doctors also have a *mutti* which is bad.

From the time I was about nine years old, I wanted to know everything about witchcraft (we call it *mutti*) and become a witch doctor.

My mother was good but very harsh. She told me not to go very deep with the witches of my country. I must love my people, but not go with the witches, because my father was a man of religion. She joined my father in his religion, so I lived as a religious person. I did go to the native school, without the consent of my mother and father, and was initiated by circumcision. The people of Boshok used to circumcise. After you had been circumcised—usually at about age twelve to sixteen, but up to age twenty—you were a man. After initiation, you also had a new name.

I went by night with a friend to the initiation place, which was by the mountain, away from the village and the people. Before you go in the door, you must have a sign, but I just went in, because I didn't understand the rules. The two men who were guarding nearly killed me for that. Because I was sixteen, they thought I was already circumcised and should be able to say the password. They fought with me, trying to push me outside, while I tried to push them inside. They tried to hit me with a knob. So I explained that I was a man who had never been circumcised. "I don't know anything," I told them. They believed me. "Why didn't you tell us that before?" they asked.

I slept there until morning, because the initiation started when the sun came up.

They taught me their law. They taught me the password. After I had been circumcised, they took me to a separate place, where I stood for an hour till the bleeding stopped.

From there we went out to train ourselves in the bush, looking for wild animals. Then we came back, to sleep. In the early morning, our eldest brothers came with food and water, and we ate. They came again with food in the evening.

We stayed in a long hut, like a tent, for three months. We hunted every day. I caught about twenty-one baboons on land where they were eating the farmers' corn. We killed them with *knobkaries*, which are long sticks with a knob on the end.

After three months, we returned home and lived the law of the men. When you are a man, you mustn't fight, you mustn't take somebody's wife, and so on.

When I went to school in Zebedal, I went by the hedge of the land and there prayed. I wanted God to reveal something to me. If something was a secret, I must understand it. But there was no answer. From then on, my heart looked deeper into the word of God. I started to understand the scriptures a little bit.

Then when I was about sixteen, I joined the company of a naughty young man. I became a champion dancer of what we call *ndebele* [custom dancing], and people awarded me for dancing. I wore African dress and then put something on my legs, to make a noise when I stomped my feet on the ground. There were nine of us dancers, including one we called the *klavle*. We used drums and an instrument like a long flute. I did this from age fifteen through eighteen.

One Sunday when I was dancing, my cousin whispered to others, "This man can dance, but he doesn't go to church, even though his father is a clergyman in the Methodist church. Today is Sunday, and he is making a nice dance here."

My heart was shocked by that.

One day a few years later, I heard of somebody who was a priest in the Twelve Apostolic Church of Zion, so I went to a night meeting. The man who preached told the congregation, "If a man doesn't repent and be baptized, he will die. Christ will kill him."

"Okay," he said, "tomorrow we will baptize you."
I was twenty-two years old.

At that time, I had the habits of smoking and drinking. After my baptism, I smoked one cigarette and gave the others to someone else. I left drinking and smoking from that time on.

When I started to read the scriptures, I wondered why there were things in my church that weren't in the scriptures. When I talked to the minister, he told me, "If you don't do as I do, then you'd better go away from my church." Then one day he came to me and said, "I don't want you. You must go out from this church."

I think it was because I had been reading the Bible, and when he did certain things, like asking us to make animal offerings to our ancestors, I would say, "The Bible doesn't agree with those things."

Then I joined a group known as the Full Gospel. It was all right. They also tried to read the scriptures, and I learned more. But one day there was a problem with garments. The garment of the wife of the minister had decorations, and the garments of other women didn't have so many, or they were different. When I studied the scriptures, I found that the special garment should go to the woman who knows the scriptures, and the minister's wife didn't read the scriptures. When I told them that, they expelled me from the church.

Another problem was that when they baptized they put people three times in the water, once in the name of the Father, once in the name of the Son, and once in the name of the Holy Spirit. The Bible doesn't teach that. "This church has been doing baptisms like this for a long time," they said. "You'd better go away."

I collected two men from that church, and we started our own church, the Generation Church of Christ. One of the men was our minister, the other the deacon, and I stood as a prophet.

The people came to us. We also made a white robe, which I didn't like, but I didn't object. People came to us until 1948, when we disorganized.

When I was in this church, my father wrote me a letter and said, "What we want you to do is find yourself a wife whom you want to marry." I was supposed to marry a cousin my father had chosen, but she was young and didn't want to marry me; she thought I was too old. So my father wrote me, "You can have anyone whom you want to marry."

I baptized Elizabeth and then married her. My father sent my eldest brother and a cousin, who brought the money for the *lobola* [dowry] and went for Elizabeth. The *lobola* was eighty pounds, but included no cattle.

I then established what I called a Church of Christ, which went on for about three years. We had a library, and I attracted people who read the scriptures as I read them, people who didn't depend on special garments but only on the Bible.

I had desires to find God and to receive revelation, but I was never satisfied, until I got the Book of Mormon. When I got the Book of Mormon and read it, I felt very good. I think it was my cousin, Brother Lekgwti, who brought a copy of the Book of Mormon, though he didn't tell me about it. I just found it in the church library.

I started to read it, then put it aside. I told my brothers, "I've read this book. It is very fine." The other ministers also read it and said it was all right, but they did not want to read it in front of the people, only separately, as ministers.

I continued to read the Book of Mormon. "It is very good," I told my brothers. "We fight every day over what the Bible says about baptism. We fight about the name of the church. The Book of Mormon is very clear on these points, and on the sacrament. People will have no need to fight if they read both the Bible and the Book of Mormon."

"Well, we can read it, but not in public," they said to me.

"This must be public, because now we have found the history of the people of America, and we have got another prophet—we have a prophet in America."

Then one day in 1964 my brethren, Isakai Manasha and Peter Mafora, came by Bertrams and saw a chapel of The Church of Jesus Christ of Latter-day Saints. They came and told me, "We saw here in Bertrams the church that speaks about the Book of Mormon."

"I'm going to look at it," I said. The next day, when I woke up, I went to the church and found nobody there.

The second time I went, I found Sister Maureen Van Zyl. "Who can I get in touch with?" I asked her. While she was giving me an address, the missionaries came to the chapel. They took me to the mission president, President Badger, who asked me, "What is your trouble?"

I explained to him, "I am with the Church of Christ, like you; you are the Church of Jesus Christ. I want to unite these two churches to be one."

"Have you been baptized?" he asked me.

"Yes, I have been baptized."

"How were you baptized?"

I told him.

"When you were baptized, did you receive the Holy Spirit? And where did the person who baptized you get the authority?"

"Well, we read the Bible."

He told me it was not like that, and then he read me the testimony of Joseph Smith.

"Okay, now you can baptize me," I said.

"If you want to be baptized, I will have to make application to Pretoria, because we can't baptize black people if it is against the law of the land."

The authorities told him, "You can teach the people, but you cannot stay in Soweto. You can only go into Soweto to teach him. We agree that you can baptize this man."

Four of us men came to Houghton and studied until we finished the lessons. In Soweto, we four men and a couple of women and children met every Sunday, and sometimes on Thursdays, to talk about going to The Church of Jesus Christ of Latter-day Saints.

One of the things that most impressed me was the lineage of authority from Jesus Christ through the Apostles to us today. The authority had been restored.

The law of chastity also impressed me, because when I was a young man, the devil tracked me to a lot of wrong ways. I kept all the other commandments, but the law of chastity was very difficult for me. When I learned about the Church and its teachings, I became a very good man. I thereafter kept the law of chastity.

The day before I was to be baptized, President Badger learned from America that the gospel was to be preached first to the whites in South Africa, and then to the blacks.

"What are we going to do?" I asked him.

"I don't know what to do, because I tried to baptize you, but now I can't go against instructions. You will have to be like the good man Cornelius, who waited to receive the word of God and become a member of the Church until after the Jews had a chance, and angels came to tell him what to do."

My friends and I waited fourteen years, until President Dale LeBaron called us and said, "Now the time is arrived for you to be baptized and come into the Church. Everything is open for you to come now. Come with your families."

I was very glad that day, very happy and excited. I came with Frans Lekgwti to see President LeBaron. He told us that we must never go back, but go forward, because the Church is the true church. He said that God had told the missionaries not to stop at the whites, but to bring in the blacks. We have not forgotten that day.

President Kimball's picture was on the wall of President LeBaron's office.

I called my friends to tell them to come to the chapel, and we started going to church. We were assigned missionaries and started the lessons. After we completed the lessons and had interviews, we went to the baptismal font and were baptized.

We received the priesthood at this time. We must understand the covenant and not play with the word of God, as our forefathers did, till God cursed them. We are no longer cursed, but are right.

I knew every mission president from President Badger to President LeBaron. President Thorn and President Clark served between those two. I got pamphlets and copies of the Book of Mormon from them and read them to my friends. Because I was known by people of the Church of Christ, I went to different places and had meetings. I gave people copies of the Book of Mormon and the pamphlets, and told them how good and true the Church was. In my heart I knew the Church was true, and that there was no other true church.

I was a great missionary. Some people even called me a witch *Masangu*. "He is a great man of the East, a king," they said. My grandfather was a king; my brother is a king and chief. We've got plenty of *Masangus* in the family. I am called "*Masangu* of the book." Some people fight with me about the Book of Mormon; others say that this book is number one.

It was not difficult to wait to be baptized, because from the time I received the teachings of the Church, almost everything became clear to me. When I thought about the sight of the Church, I became glad and forgot about things that were not good. I was very happy.

From that time in 1978, some of us from Soweto began attending church in the Johannesburg chapel. Then in 1982 we began a branch in Soweto. We are now a branch of more than a hundred people in Soweto.

My wife had not been involved with the Church before, but after I was baptized, if I said but one word to my wife, she would reply, "Yes, I will go with you to the church." Then she said to me, "I want to be a member also in that church, because now I see it is true." None of my children will say they don't like the Church. Even my adopted son, when I told him about the Church, said, "All right, I will be there."

When I became a member, I was very weak. I had nothing in my house. I had not held a job for two years. After I joined the Church, everything came easier, and I got a job.

I feel the power of God in my body, through the priesthood. When I went to the temple, I felt like a man who had just woken up from death. Today I am in a certain place in my life, but I see steps and other steps and still other steps. Going to the temple with my wife was a higher step.

The Church of Jesus Christ of Latter-day Saints is true. You can read about it in the Bible, and even more clearly in the Book of Mormon. The Doctrine and Covenants contains the scriptures that point at us, the new people of this generation. And the Pearl of Great Price is also an important book. These are the standards of the Church.

In the time of Joseph Smith, God brought the Church of Jesus Christ into the sun, where everybody could see it. It is true. Our Heavenly Father lives and has a body of flesh and bone. Jesus Christ is his Son. Joseph Smith was a prophet, and from Joseph Smith to Ezra Taft Benson there have been true prophets in our time.

18

Erna Raikes

Live in Harmony, Despite Differences

Erna Raikes, a mixed-blood South African, struggled with feelings of bitterness because of imposed laws which limited her freedoms. Through finding the gospel she discovered the true and complete source to freedom and happiness. Erna now has a new appreciation and gratitude for her heritage. She was born in 1943 in Wynbert, South Africa. In 1970 she married Emil Raikes, and they have one son, Carl. She worked for fourteen years as a secretary and for six years as a model. She was baptized on 6 July 1986.

I was born of mixed parents, the eldest of three sisters. (One brother died before I was born.) My father was actually white, born of a St. Helenan father and an English mother. My mother's father was English and her mother was so-called colored, though also from St. Helenan stock.

My father made the decision that we should be classified as colored, though this was always a bone of contention with my sisters. He did not want us to be humiliated. He feared we might get married and have one dark child, and the others white; and that child would be victimized. He would not want us to suffer that.

Once I was a bit late, so I rushed onto a train, which I could not afford to miss. I entered the white section and was told to move along through the eight white coaches to the coach for coloreds, even though all these white coaches were empty. (There are usually eight or nine empty white coaches before the one first-class colored coach, even though we pay the same fare as the whites do.)

I said, "But I pay the same as these people, and this coach is empty."

"Sorry, lady. It is not my rule. You have to get on the colored coach."

"What shall I do?" I asked. "I have to travel only a short distance, and I'll be at my destination before I get to the colored coach. Why can't I just sit here?"

"It's against the law."

So, terribly humiliated, I had to walk through eight coaches.

As I tried to get into the colored coach, it was so crowded that I had to battle to get in. I wasn't quite into the coach when the conductor blew his whistle. "Why are you doing this?" I asked him. "We are not in yet!"

He replied in Afrikaans, "You are a lot of sheep, there are so many of you. You are a lot of sheep."

A colored man said, "If I were white and a conductor, I would still be a 'sheep'. How dare you call only us 'sheep'? If we were white and had the authority, you wouldn't be a train conductor."

We resented being called sheep.

When I complained to authorities about the lack of coaches for coloreds, they said I should simply take another train.

"How can I take another train? How would I get home? Why aren't there more colored coaches?" I demanded.

"Have less children. There are too many of you."

I can't describe the humiliation I suffered.

I also remember, as a little girl, about six or seven years old, going to the pool. My sister, who was fairer than I was, said, "Come along to this pool." But I stood and wouldn't go. My dad asked, "Erna, why aren't you going into the pool?"

"I don't want to," I replied.

"Come on. Why don't you want to come?"

"Because I see a Whites Only sign there."

I was afraid of being victimized and embarrassed. I didn't want any policeman coming to me and saying, "I'm sorry, but you are too black. Would you please get out of the pool."

My father couldn't force me. My sisters were splashing away, because they knew that nobody would query them about being in the pool because of their color.

I have really suffered.

My memories of early childhood are quite confusing, actually, because I was of mixed parents, went to separate schools, and got into separate trains.

My father said there was nothing he could do about the problem. He had to abide by the rules of our country at all costs, no matter how we resented them. He did specify that we should not feel any lesser or inferior because of this. They were not his laws, but the country's laws.

Yet it always worried me. My sisters were fairer than I, and when one of them was about sixteen, she actually used to get in the white coaches. Being fair, she met with no objection—until my father found out. He really gave her a talking to; he said that if her sisters could get in a colored coach, and so could he, then so could she. My father stopped her as well from getting a white ID card, which she would have had no problem doing. She eventually married a man of mixed color.

Once, when I was about fourteen, my sister and I had a big flare-up; she said to me, "You are black." My father stepped in and said, "I don't ever want to hear you say that again. Don't ever talk to your sister like that. Being darker doesn't mean she is a lesser person than you. There is nothing wrong with being black."

There are coloreds that are sometimes whiter than the whites, though they are termed "colored" and go to colored schools and get in colored coaches. This is changing now, but basically, that's how it used to be.

My primary school was termed "colored." My school experience was quite successful. I was in many activities—tap dancing, ballet, Greek, Spanish, and Russian; and speech and drama, in which I did very well.

My sisters both emigrated to Australia. My father visited them shortly after they moved, and he loved it. He said that if he weren't so old, he would definitely emigrate. My son Carl and I visited as well, and you could feel the difference. People were helpful in the buses and trains, and very friendly. They didn't think less of us because we were slightly darker. There was no color difference. Such an atmosphere made me feel good.

But I was born in South Africa, and I don't feel I should go away. I belong here. I should endure what the others are enduring. Why should I be a coward and go away? There is no point in running away. I am proud of what I am, being classified "mixed" or "colored." I do find it derogatory, but I am not ashamed of what I am, and I tell my son this every day.

Erna Raikes

Color means nothing. It is just pigmentation. It doesn't change the person. In fact, the word *colored* can mean several different things: It can mean anything from being a colored who might look like an African, to being snow white; or it might mean being totally black, with kinky hair and hard features, or what have you. To me, it means nothing.

Still, I have had many humiliating experiences. Now I make it my business to go only places where everyone can go. My son became aware of discrimination at a very early age.

I met my husband, Emil, when I was nineteen, and we married nine years later. Emil has serious mental problems, and sometimes these become very tough to deal with, especially for our son. Actually, I was told by my husband's psychiatrist not to have children, because of Emil's problems.

I do know that my Heavenly Father knows why I married Emil. I have been faithful to Emil, though it has been difficult. If I continually pray and have faith in my Heavenly Father, he will help me. I am enduring, though Emil is deteriorating very rapidly.

I sometimes feel it is unfair of me to let Carl experience this hardship, but he insists on being faithful to his father. Emil came from a very unstable family.

I went to Sunday school from age three, and enjoyed it. My mother encouraged it. I was active in two different churches, but actually belonged to the church group where I did Bible study.

Two things bothered me. I was very puzzled about life after death. We were told simply that our "souls would go to heaven," which wasn't ever clear to me. Would I be Erna, or would my mother be my mother? Would souls just float around heaven? Heaven, to me, was something very vague.

And I hadn't been baptized by immersion. My Bible study teacher said that immersion wasn't necessary. I replied, "Well, John the Baptist baptized by immersion, so I know that you've got to be baptized that way." I didn't get a satisfactory answer from him. I also didn't feel strong fellowship in that church.

I actually started staying away from church, going only once a month, rather than once a week, though I did keep in touch.

What I never stopped doing was praying, which I had been encouraged to do from when I was little. When my son was born, we did this as well, praying together from when he was at a very early age. I also sent him to church. He never missed a Sunday. I explained to him nicely about the scriptures, and about baptism as well.

He asked me, "Mom, why aren't you baptized?"

"We are going to be baptized," I told him. "It's just that I'm not happy with churches anymore, but I know that we are going to be baptized."

This was about the time that the missionaries came along. I think we were actually waiting for them. It was my husband who invited them around. He was at the supermarket, and they asked him if they could come to his home. He told them they could.

So my husband told me that some people were coming, but he wasn't very specific. I had an appointment. "If you can't be honest with me and tell me who these people are, then I won't be here. I've got to know who they are!"

I was about to leave, when the missionaries walked in. I didn't realize who they were or what church they were from. The name "The Church of Jesus Christ of Latter-day Saints" didn't mean a thing to me. I didn't associate it with the Mormons.

I had heard about Mormons, but what I heard wasn't true— that they could have as many wives as they wanted. I didn't investigate, because I didn't believe in that.

After my appointment I rushed back to the house quickly, but, unfortunately, the missionaries had left. Carl was very impressed by what they had to say. I said to him, "If you were impressed, I am eager to hear what they have to say. Maybe it will solve this problem we have about your baptism. Maybe our prayers will be answered."

Carl phoned the missionaries that very night and told them to come back the next day, or the day after. I requested that they show me the film *The First Vision*, which had so impressed Carl. Carl had said that Joseph Smith was in the same dilemma as we were, wanting to know which church was right. My parents had wanted Carl to be confirmed in one church, and were asking about his going to yet another church.

The missionaries returned, and I saw the film. I was impressed. They left some pamphlets. I didn't question the missionaries too much.

I did say to Carl, "I have a feeling that these people are Mormons."

"Mom, what are Mormons?"

"Carl, it may not be true, but I have heard that they can have as many wives as they choose. That violates a commandment. I will have to look into this before you become too excited."

When the missionaries came around again, the first thing I asked them was about the many wives. They answered my questions and explained the Book of Mormon.

After about two weeks, I decided that this was what I was looking for. The concepts of the Bible that were vague to me were all clarified by the Book of Mormon. That is how I came to know it was another testament of Jesus Christ. It was like a jigsaw puzzle —everything fit into the right place. I know the Book of Mormon is true.

Carl actually discovered that before I did. He said that when he saw the film *The First Vision*, he had a "cold feeling." He said he felt something cold go through him.

I said to him, "Carl, that is the Holy Spirit." He wanted me to experience that same feeling, which I actually had not felt at that time. I had been impressed, but hadn't had the same feeling. It only hit me afterwards, after I said to myself, "No way am I going to let Carl influence me. I want to experience it myself." There has been no looking back since.

What I especially loved was the fellowship, and I think that this is what Emil enjoyed initially, because I don't think he could comprehend the gospel. I was worried that he simply liked the people, so we waited two months to be baptized. I wanted to make sure that Emil made a right decision for himself. He enjoys church very much.

I think what most impressed me about the Church was that I finally knew where I was going. I was no longer vague about where my soul would go. I knew exactly where it would go if I obeyed the commandments and was baptized. That gave me a good feeling, because this question had worried me since I was a child.

Initially, I couldn't stop reading. I found more and more truths, the more I read. I think this was because of my background in churches and Bible study. The Book of Mormon alone was sufficient for Carl. Fortunately, he now takes seminary, and he says, "Everything is fitting, and I can see now why you study the Bible, because you can see how the Book of Mormon shows that it is definitely true."

I was overwhelmed by my baptism. I knew that whatever adversities I might have, in my married life, especially, my Heavenly Father would help me endure. He has planned my life on earth, so whatever I endure is what he wanted me to endure, and I know he will see me through to the end.

Carl and I have a fantastic relationship. He is very protective towards me because of his father's condition. "I will do everything for you," he says.

I tell him, "No, you don't have to. I have you, and you are a joy to me, and you help me in whatever I do."

Carl is diligent in whatever he does, in sports and in school. He gets top grades. He's a top sportsman. He isn't conceited. He tries hard to do his best in whatever he does, and, fortunately, he is very talented.

The Church has been a ray of hope to Emil. Without the Church, he might have gone under, because he didn't have a very good spiritual background. We cling to the hope the gospel gives. Studying the scriptures may help him overcome the affliction he has.

The greatest change in me is that I don't feel sorry for myself anymore. People think I am a martyr to endure what I do, but I know it was meant to be.

The sisters in Relief Society are wonderful. They uplift me. We share our problems, and this helps with my burdens. By listening to their problems, you wonder why you are complaining—so many people have major problems. You have the support of the sisters all the time.

The majority of my friends and family are horrified about us joining the Church. Most of them think of themselves as reborn Christians, and they believe we are a sect. They have so much anti-Mormon literature, nothing we say or do can change their minds. I admire Carl for standing up for what he believes. He has never, ever denied his church or his faith, in spite of teachers who have actually ridiculed him.

He says he wants to explain his church to people. I tell him he doesn't have to convince people himself. What he has to do is explain and bear testimony

"Mom," he tells me, "this is what I want to do one day—to help convince people." And I know that he will do that one day.

I would tell people who are interested in my life story that they must never deny their heritage. They must be proud of what they are, and not wish to be of another species or race. Our Heavenly Father has sent us here, and he has reason for us to endure all our problems, maybe so that in the future we can all live in harmony, despite differences in the pigmentation of our skin.

I would tell whoever is interested, not to deny our church, not to deny our Heavenly Father. The Book of Mormon is another testament of Jesus Christ. By studying it and the other scriptures, by praying, by having faith, by being diligent, by obeying the commandments, by being an example, we can be helpful to others.

19

Dolly Henrietta Ndhlovu

Come and Follow Jesus Christ

Dolly Henrietta Ndhlovu was born in 1921 in Escort, Natal, South Africa, and being the oldest of ten children, was responsible for caring for the cattle and doing other farm chores. Her father was a school principal and a preacher. Through great sacrifice Dolly completed her education to become a nurse and made nursing her career. She married Andrew Ndhlovu in 1955, and they had one son. She joined the Church in 1984. The gospel has brought great blessings into her life, including the joy of temple worship.

My father was a farmer, and a very busy man. My mother used to do a lot of the farm work too.

When I was very small my mother, when cooking, would lay me on the floor, because we had no beds. She would light a candle and put it just above my head, for light, and then she would start her cooking. One night when it was late, I lifted my hand, and the candle fell on me. The blankets got burnt, and so did my forehead. I understand it was a terrible burn. There were no hospitals or other help except the Lutheran priest. He treated me.

My mother and father had ten children, five boys and five girls. The five boys all died at birth or in their youth. Two of the girls also died in their youth.

As my father had no boys or anybody older than me, when I was six or seven years old, I had to look after the cattle and bring them along and hand them over to him. I did that every day of my life until I finished my standard six [eighth grade] in school at about age fifteen.

Boys who were watching their cattle used to fight me and think I was stubborn. At times they used sticks. I fought them, even though I was short. I would take stones and hit them.

At school, the teacher, who was very strict, used to punish me by hitting me. Then in the afternoon when I got home, I would tell my father, who was a very active member of the school committee and who helped much in church. He went and talked to the teacher.

My father was a good friend of the teacher, who was also the principal at the time, but my father made it a little difficult for me, because the teachers would say, "Dolly Henrietta can never be thrashed, because obviously her father will be here in no time." I used to work closely with my father. We looked after the cattle together. We used to do the plowing. Then every afternoon or evening we would go back and demand food at home. My mother was the cook, but she was also very busy in the fields with us during the day. When she had a small child, she would put the child under the trees and let the child sleep there.

My parents were very good members of their church. My father was a preacher in the church and had quite a lot of work allocated to him. My mother was also very active. She belonged to the mothers' union of the church, and they used to meet on Thursdays and do church work.

I used to be very scared of snakes, as most Africans are. I think it is the education we have from our religious heritage. My parents, when they read the Bible, said that the snake was a very terrible thing. They associated the snake with Satan. "You must always be careful of a snake. He will eat your heel, and you will not be able to walk." I would never hit a snake, just run. I was told that when you run, the snake can run over the grass and catch you. Even today, when I get home, I look around the corners and under my bed, to make sure there are no snakes.

I also look for *tsotzies*—a type of people who break into houses, hooligans.

In 1935 my father became very ill and couldn't do much of anything. He sold the place he had bought, bundled us up, and moved to a new place. He left quite a lot of his valuables behind—cows, horses, sheep, and so on—under somebody's care. Also, he left one special article that he and my mother honored—the Bible.

After six months, our former home in Escort was burnt, and everything in the house was burnt. My father was worried about his Bible that he had left behind—the Bible that our father and mother had been teaching us out of.

At the new place, I went to school near Durban. I had to restart my standard six [eighth grade]. The coming year I went to Inanda Seminary, where I continued with my junior certificate classes. During this time, it was very difficult for my father, because he had never before been stranded and without money. He was not doing any of his farming business, and he had a real tough time.

My teachers wanted me to take up teaching, but I said I was too short, even shorter than my students would be. (I am only four feet eleven inches tall.) "I would rather take nursing," I said. I was very interested in nursing. I have a soft heart for sick people. So my teachers recommended me to do nursing in Durban, near my home.

I loved nursing. I loved my patients. I mostly loved children. I used to sing when tending the children, and even when I was nursing others. The patients would say, "My wound must be dressed by that little nurse in training because I feel happy as she does the dressing and sings."

I completed my general nursing in 1943. My family had left Durban by then. I was really glad when I got the results from my exams. When you are waiting for exams, you don't know how you have done, especially in nursing, because the nursing exam is very difficult. My parents couldn't read English, so I said to my mother, "Mama, if my results come and I am not here, please look at the first letter. If it is a C, for 'congratulations,' then you will know that I have passed."

I wasn't at home when the results came. My mother saw me coming from far off and went out on the veranda, laughing as I came along. I wondered what she was laughing about; I didn't think the results were out. She showed me the letter, and when I asked what was written, she said, "C."

I was pleased and grateful that I had passed my exams and would be able to help my parents, because they were really in need.

I applied to work in the general hospital in Johannesburg. The matron put me on pension, without me knowing what pension was. (Being on pension means that you put money away monthly, for when you retire.) I was allocated to the babies, because I said I liked babies.

Whatever envelope I was given at the end of the month, I took to my father first. I would never open it.

In 1946 the matron of the nurses allowed me to study for midwifery. I went to Durban and trained for a year, then came back and continued to work where I had started.

In 1947 the general hospital was moved to Paragoinat and became one of the biggest hospitals in South Africa. In 1948 I was promoted to senior sister, which meant that I was in charge of a few wards. I later became a matron.

I continued to work until 1981, when I was old enough to be pensioned. I retired and left the hospital and went into private nursing. I've worked in a Jewish old-age home since December 1981.

I met my husband, Andrew Ndhlovu, at the Paragoinat Hospital, where he was a clerk. He was a widower with four small children. I was thirty-four years old when I got married. I got married late because I thought my first responsibility was to look after my parents and help them meet their needs.

In three years, I had my own child, Christian Ndhlovu Mandla. He lived with my cousin in Swaziland and was brought up a staunch Catholic. After my husband died, my son asked me if I would join him in his church. "It is best for us to be together," he said.

Christian has gone to school in Canada, and is now doing his master's degree in electrical engineering in California.

My sister and her daughter joined The Church of Jesus Christ of Latter-day Saints. One day my sister phoned me to say I must look for her daughter, Alphinia, because she was near me with "the Church."

"What church?" I asked.

"The Church of Jesus Christ of Latter-day Saints."

"But what a long name! What is this that you have joined now?"

My sister asked me to look for the daughter, but when I went to find her, she was out touring. On my way from the church back to town, four European students, who were from the same conference as my niece and were going to town, asked me who I wanted and where I was going. "We will give you a lift as far as Soweto," they said.

On the way, one of the students said to me, "Do you belong to the Church?"

"No, I don't belong to 'the Church.' I have my own church. I am an Anglican."

She asked me if I would like to know more about the Church.

"I don't mind," I answered. "You can tell me about the Church."

She asked if I would mind having the elders come to my home to tell me about the Church.

I told her that anyone could come to my house. I welcomed anybody. I would like to listen to the elders.

She promised to send the two elders who usually come to Soweto.

So I waited for the elders.

One of them phoned to tell me they were coming soon to tell me about the Church. Would I allow them to come?

"Yes, with pleasure, come." But I was doing night duty, and they couldn't come when I was free.

After a month or so, when I was also again working nights, I heard a knock on the door. I saw two tall, nice-looking young men standing there. "Oh," I thought. "It must be those missionaries that lady said she was going to send me."

They told me they were the elders.

"What can I do for you?"

They said they understood that I would like to know more about The Church of Jesus Christ of Latter-day Saints.

"Yes, I'll be going to work soon. Next week I'll be free."

They made an appointment, but they couldn't find my place again. People always miss it.

Finally they came and started to tell me about the Church. Then they wanted to know if they could come back.

"Oh, yes. Come back."

I decided to get my neighbors to come and listen too. Two of them came the next time.

The missionaries had left me a copy of the Book of Mormon and wanted to know if I had read it.

"No, I haven't read it, but I will read it when I've got time."

They made another appointment, and four neighbors came. So the missionaries started again from the beginning of the lessons. The neighbors were not prepared to come back, because they were busy. So I remained alone with the elders.

They asked me questions that did not register with me. I hadn't read anything, and I didn't remember what the elders had been talking about.

The elders were quite patient. They started again at the beginning and gave me some verses to read. I didn't read them. At the next appointment I had to tell them again that I hadn't read anything.

The elders kept on coming. They asked me to pray to understand the Book of Mormon.

Then I started reading and praying. As I started reading the

Book of Mormon, I felt something in me, and I saw that I could read the book without stopping. At times I would get up at two in the morning to read. It was so interesting to me that I found myself reading it continuously. I just felt I belonged to this book. Something told me I belonged to this organization.

My worry was how to tell my priest that I belonged to another church. How would that work?

The elders invited me to come to church—to come and listen. At the time, a conference was coming up in East Rand.

Fortunately I was working, so I had an excuse not to go. I had to rest during the day. "I work twelve hours a day, and I work very hard," I told the elders.

But they sacrificed to leave town to come and fetch me in Soweto and take me to East Rand, and from East Rand take me to work. So I prepared myself for the conference.

When I first attended church, I saw only a few people, and I said, "Where are all the people of this church? So few means this church is not understood."

Still I felt that the Book of Mormon and also the pamphlets I had read were saying something to me. Something said I should make up my mind: I must choose between the Anglican church and what I had read and understood concerning the Church.

I prayed, and I think the Lord answered me, because I felt I needn't go to the Anglican church anymore. I must go to the new church and understand what it was all about. Even at work I continued reading, if I had a little bit of time.

The elders were helpful in explaining what I didn't understand.

Then they introduced the matter of baptism. I asked them, "Is it necessary that one should be baptized again, if one has been baptized when young?"

They answered, "Yes, it is necessary."

I prayed about this but couldn't see why one should be baptized a second time. Then one night I thought about it and said to myself, "What is wrong with being baptized for the second time?"

My sister would phone me and tell me that she had been baptized and felt very happy about it. Her children also felt very happy. And if I joined the Church, we would become closer and communicate well.

I continued to pray about it, until one day I decided I should be baptized. I was baptized on 18 March 1984.

I invited quite a lot of relatives to my baptism. They came, including my sister, who wanted to see me baptized.

I felt I now belonged to the right place. As I went down in the water, I felt as though something was taking me somewhere, to a place nobody knows, but a very safe place. I felt very happy about it. When the elders put their hands on my head, I felt I didn't belong to this world, but to another world. I felt that somehow the world was not for me. I must work for the Lord.

I see a lot of change in myself. I didn't used to go to church every Sunday, but since I joined the Church, I have never felt that I wouldn't go to church. I've always felt that is my first responsibility. I feel as though something has made me clean. Quite a lot of things I used to be interested in come secondary now. Instead of doing some of the things that are not productive, I would rather sit and read Church books.

When I got my patriarchal blessing, I felt I had a duty to do certain things. The only trouble with me is that I am always short of words. I always feel depressed about my failing to say what I want to say, and instead just saying part of what I want to say. Some of the most important things that I want to say, I always fail to say. I feel like Enoch and Moses must have felt, but those two were blessed, because God was with them. He talked to them and fed them with words that he wanted them to say.

I saw the temple in Johannesburg from the onset, when it was being put up, and I was told it was our temple. I first came when it was dedicated in August of 1985. My sister from Durban was there. We were all excited to be able to go into the temple. I felt very happy, as though I didn't belong to this world anymore. I wished that people from Soweto and town would also know about the temple, and have the privilege to come and see and hear what was being taught there.

Now I go to the temple every two weeks, because in my work I have one week off, one week on. I am able to do the work for those people who have passed away but were not able to be baptized, receive their endowments, and be sealed.

I would like to call upon everybody to listen to the gospel message and come and follow Jesus Christ. He is there for all of us. He will accept us with all his might. As we follow him, we will always have the wonderful home that he has promised us.

I would also like to say to my people, especially in Soweto, to listen to the voices of the elders when they come. People's spirits will be cleansed, and they will be highly delighted to hear about the Church. It has been restored through our Father's prophet, Joseph Smith. If we follow all the Lord's sayings, we will never run away from following his example.

20

Alice Johanna Okkers

I Would Love to Touch the Door of the Temple

Alice Johanna Okkers, born on 12 May 1900 in Cape Town, South Africa, is the daughter of one of the first colored people of South Africa to accept the gospel. Sister Okkers's father, William Paul Daniels, was baptized in Utah in 1915, so she grew up with faithful Latter-day Saint parents. Sister Okkers was baptized into the Church in 1920, and she was seventy-eight years of age when the priesthood revelation was received, making it possible for her to go to the temple for herself as well as for her beloved parents. She married Pieter Okkers in 1944, and they had one daughter. Alice Okkers is a faithful sister with a rich heritage.

I had good earthly parents. They were good and loving and made sure that in our home we served the Lord, morning, night, and noon. Every morning, we would hear my father's favorite hymn: "Do what is right; let the consequence follow."

I don't know about my parents' courtship. I know my mother used to work at the castle, as a maid for the admiral. My father used to meet her outside the castle, when she went home.

We were brought up very strictly. When people came to our home, our parents just gave us a big look, and we disappeared into the yard. My father was a very staunch and faithful deacon in the Dutch Reformed church for sixteen years. Then something happened that offended him. He left that church.

One of the elders from The Church of Jesus Christ of Latter-day Saints later came to his house and preached the gospel. So my father made up his mind that he would join that church.

My father and his two sons, Able and Simon, went over to Salt Lake City the year the *Titanic* sunk, just before World War I. They stayed there eight months. All were baptized there.

Then the war broke out, so my mother said to my father that he must come home and not forget to bring her two sons back.

While he was in Salt Lake City, he went to the Church and said he so much wanted to hold the priesthood. David O. McKay told him, "Don't worry, Brother Daniels. If you don't hold the priesthood on earth, you will hold it in heaven."

Before returning to Africa, my father was given a blessing by the President of the Church, Joseph F. Smith, who promised him that someday he would hold the priesthood, if he lived faithfully. That blessing meant so much to my father that he would cry when he spoke about it.

When my father returned to South Africa, he wanted very much to take an active part in the Church, as he had done in his former church. But he was very disappointed. He talked to President Dalton, the president of the South African mission, who told him the same thing as David O. McKay and President Smith. President Dalton was very fond of my father.

So my father went back to his home and told my mother, "I don't think I'll go to church anymore." He was that disappointed.

Mother coached him: "Listen, you have been over to Salt Lake City and been baptized."

He turned to her and said, "All right, I'll go to church."

On Monday nights, the elders used to come up to our place. We had something to eat together and then had a little meeting. We studied *Jesus the Christ* by James E. Talmage, and bore our testimonies.

President Dalton organized a little branch called the "Branch of Love." We were only six families together. We just had our own meetings, but no Relief Society or anything like that. We didn't have every opportunity as we have now. I didn't know very much about the gospel.

It was only in 1978 that we colored people could hold the priesthood, and that is when I became a staunch member. I am sorry to have to say that, but God knows, and I cannot lie.

My brothers left the Church.

On his deathbed, in 1936, my father bore his testimony of the Church and laid his hands on his children and blessed them. He said to me, "Alice, you are the only girl, and I know you will look after your mother. And don't forget to go to church. I am going to ask you to promise something."

"Yes?"

"Stand by the Church!"

I have stood by the Church until now, when I am at the age of eighty-eight years. I am the only one still alive of the old family. My mother, father, brothers, and sister, my baby, my husband—everyone is gone. So I am lonely.

I am very glad I am a member of this church. We members are in the world, but not of the world. We live differently and feel different. As I walk along the street, I feel different. As people look at Latter-day Saints, they see we always have smiles on our faces. Sometimes I think it is very difficult to be a Latter-day Saint, because you get all the ups and downs and knocks together, but if you have faith in the Lord Jesus Christ, and ask God to help you, he will help you.

We have a lovely chapel in the Strand, near Cape Town. We feel we are together and that the Lord is in our midst. We love it and always ask God to help us get more members in our church.

I am getting very, very old. My sight is giving in. My legs are giving out. I know that the Lord did open the windows of heaven for me, because I am still here, and everybody says they can't believe my age. When I am sick, I call on the elders to come and anoint me. I am very fond of my people. The branch president is very good to me. The Lord has blessed me wonderfully. I always pray to God that when the time comes, the Lord will come and fetch me. But as long as I live, I can be an example to my people.

I can thank the Lord that I had the opportunity of meeting one of our prophets, President Spencer W. Kimball. I met him and spoke to him face-to-face in Johannesburg, when we had an area conference. He and his counselors were there. A child came to fetch me out of the crowd and said to me, "I want Alice Daniels to come and sit right in front with the President and his counselors." So I did.

Just before the closing hymn, I was taken to a bus. We went to the Carlton Hotel and went up the lift. I met President Kimball, President N. Eldon Tanner, President Gordon B. Hinckley, and their wives.

I asked them to bless me. They put their hands on my head and also asked me about the gospel. I said I knew the gospel was the true gospel. I said I had dreamed one day that I would love to touch the door of the temple.

President Kimball said, "Don't worry. If you have the faith and the strength, the Lord will help and encourage you, and you shall reach a temple."

A voice came from somewhere and said, "The Salt Lake Temple," but I didn't answer it. I never thought that my dream could come true.

Two years later, one of the brethren in the branch brought me a ticket to Salt Lake City. I went and stayed for forty-five days. I went to the temple. I went to meetings. I did all my genealogy and temple work for my parents, my brothers, my sisters, and my husband.

After going to the temple I went and got my patriarchal blessing —a wonderful blessing, and I thank the Lord for it. I said, "God is good to me." I am the only member of the family who has received a patriarchal blessing.

When I was sealed to my parents I was very happy. I was struck dumb and went into tears—to think that our Lord would suffer, so that we could enjoy this beautiful thing! I had very nice parents, and I was glad to know they were with the Lord. I often pray for them. The temple was so wonderful, I thought that if I should close my eyes, I could be with the Lord.

I was also very anxious and sad, being alone, with not a brother or sister who could comfort me. And my color made me feel a bit like I was in an arena.

I am happy in the Church. In taking the sacrament, I always think about the sacrifice our Lord has made for us by shedding his blood for us. To be worthy to take the sacrament, to preach the gospel, and to be of help to one another are very difficult. It is also hard to be a Christian, when you kick against the pricks. Satan is so cunning. He tries to tempt you in different ways. I say, "Oh, get behind me, Satan. You are busy with me again."

The elders hold meetings in my home, and I always pray in my home. I know that the Lord hears and answers my prayers. I just wait for the time when he will come to fetch me. I will be very, very glad, but the time is not ripe yet.

Father gave his Only Begotten Son for us. I think of how an earthly father offers his missionary son for the gospel, so that we can enjoy this beautiful gospel. I ask God to bless me in the areas where I am weak. He has given me strength to have health and happiness. God is great, and I only hope that the people who come to my home, or my neighbors and friends, will hear the beautiful gospel, because they lose a lot when they know nothing about it. My patriarchal blessing tells me that I must try to preach the gospel to my people. I do.

I pray every night and morning that the Lord will hear my

prayers and help me overcome my weaknesses. I bend my knees and offer myself and ask the Lord to raise me up in the morning to thank him for the beautiful world, the sea, and everything given us that we enjoy.

The Lord has blessed me wonderfully, so that I can share. I am quite satisfied with the little I've got. I am given a pension of 174 rand a month, of which I pay one-tenth in tithing. I give my niece 88 rand for letting me live here. One week the doctor bill and my tablets and medicine came to 60 rand. I pay 3 rand fast offering and 2 rand to the missionary fund. My branch president says I needn't pay the missionary money, but I love to pay it. Though I pay only a small amount, it is better than nothing. It can help. I am very glad to think that two young girls from our branch left just last month to preach the gospel. If I get more money, I will pay more tithing. I am wonderfully blessed.

I know that people can enjoy the gospel, if they will only give up what they have to give up, and sacrifice.

21

Sello Isaac Mbele

I Began to Feel Loved

Sello Isaac Mbele, born in 1950 in Springfield, South Africa, grew up without love, support, or protection from family members. From the age of nine he was compelled to survive as best he could. In spite of incredible hardships and trials, through the healing power of the gospel he overcame emotional and spiritual scars. Through the Church and the gospel he has found joy and love. He married Lydia Matilo in 1976, and they have two children.

I was born in 1950 in Springfield, in Vereeniging. My parents never stayed together after I was born, because they didn't communicate very well. I stayed with my grandmother, my mother's mother, until I was about five or six years old.

My grandmother was good to me. She taught me how to live right. But she was already an old person. I think she died, but at that time little children normally weren't told what happened to the old people when they died. I didn't know where my mother was; she was married to another man.

The family decided to hand me over to my mother's uncle, so I went to another place to live, on a farm. Because he was older than me, my uncle's son used to treat me badly. We used to fight every day. Nobody talked to me, because I was not their son. Nobody looked after me. Sometimes I used to go to bed hungry. Sometimes I was sent to sleep outside the house. Because I was young, I didn't know what to do or where to go.

When I was about nine years old, my mother's uncle chased me away because of some problems in the family. He gave me two blankets and my shirts and said, "Go!"

I didn't know where to go, I was so young.

Traveling by foot, I went to Vereeniging, and there I started to live the wild life. I tried to look for garden work, but I couldn't get any because I was so young. I looked for empty cool-drink bottles, which I would sell for a piece of bread.

Sometimes it rained, and my blanket would get wet, and I couldn't sleep with it. I then had to go find a place to hide myself, behind buildings, in empty houses, and in other places. One time I left my blankets in the veld [prairie grass], and when I came back at night, I found somebody had put a match to the veld and burned it and my blankets, and I didn't know where to sleep. It was a terrible time. Sometimes policemen would make their searchings and catch me for trespassing. Twice I was sent to a home for young children who don't have parents to look after them.

Two or three days after my blankets burned, I found an empty cardboard box and put one part underneath me and one on top of me. Nobody cared for me, and nobody loved me. As I said, I started to go wild. I even hated people. I used to fight with people older than I, if I thought I could get their money. I managed to defend myself. Everyone was my enemy.

I became just a crook, a criminal. I began to take people's money without their agreement. I stole things.

I don't want any child of mine to live the same life I lived.

An Indian man offered me a job cleaning buggies or cars and going with him to pick up flowers to sell. I used to sleep in his empty shop.

When I reached the age for getting my identity [card], at sixteen years, I began to feel bad. Then my uncle came to look for me. I went and lived with him, but unfortunately, it was nearly the same as when I lived with him before. My uncle would cane me and say I was stubborn, if I didn't do everything I was told. I was always hating. Everyone was my enemy.

Then I went away again. I tried to find work, but I couldn't because I didn't have a permit. This was during the time of influx control; you had to have a passbook to work.

So again I was on a lot of travels. I thought I was okay because I had a reference book, but I didn't have a work permit. The police were always catching me. I didn't work.

The police sent me to the police station, and from there I was sent to jail for about two or three months' imprisonment. We were "sold" to the farmers to work on their farms, where we would make bricks, or look after cattle. I don't know how many times I went to jail—more than twenty, sometimes for ten days, sometimes for more.

I became more wild and cocky. One farmer bought us, but we fled from him at night. It happened like this: On that farm we slept on grain bags; there were no blankets. One night I set an empty bag alight. The other prisoners woke up and saw the big light. The watchman outside opened the door to see what everybody was yelling about. That is when we fled.

I wasn't free for long before I was caught by the police again. I got another punishment for what I did.

I also used to be a gambler, with playing cards, dice, cocks, and things like that.

Then I realized that this life was no good for me. I couldn't progress that way. I used to see an old man who was also living the same life that I was living. I asked myself, "Where are his children? Where is his wife?" I then made a decision that when I married, I would not leave my children, like I was left.

In 1968 I had an accident, and my hand and face were burned. I stayed in the hospital for three months.

I started a business, buying clothes from wholesalers and selling the clothes. That helped me a lot. I progressed. That is how I came to meet my wife, because now I was traveling by train and selling by train. But there were also problems, because the railway police didn't allow people to sell things on trains. We always got in trouble with the police, but at least it was a better life than I used to live.

For a while I was a bus driver, but I got dismissed and went to a nearby town to look for work. By that time, my reference book was okay, but I was only allowed to live in a hostel, not in a township. I had a temporary permit. When I went to the Department of Transit Offices to look for work, I was given the address of a man named Snyman, to see if he had a job for me.

He was different from all the other managers I used to see. He was kind. He spoke softly to me. I felt different around him, dignified.

He asked me where I had worked, and I told him the places, because they were written on my passbook. Some of them I tried to hide; I didn't want to tell him the truth.

He phoned some of the people and asked them what kind of person I was. My last boss said, "That is the last person you can give work to in Patanga. Isaac is the worst man you can give work to."

Mr. Snyman told me what they said, and asked me why I left those jobs. I explained, and he said, "Okay, we will see." I worked with him for three days. He took me for a test drive, and also sent someone else to test me. He was satisfied with me, and I worked for him for about four or five months.

His daughter Jenny had just finished serving her mission. One day she noticed me and said, "Something is wrong with Isaac today. What is wrong?"

I didn't want to tell her the truth. "Nothing." I told her just a little bit, not a lot.

I felt good with the work I was doing, and with the people around me.

It didn't take long before the thing came to me again. I couldn't pretend. She could see that something was wrong with me.

The problem was between my wife and me. I wasn't treating her as good as I should. I was not happy with my marriage or my life. I was drinking and doing other things. I was completely confused. I didn't know what to do with my life, how I could sort it out.

Then she said again, "Today I have to tell you something. I am not going to tell you the whole story, just part. Have you ever seen those two young men who used to come and visit with me?"

"Yes."

"They are good people," she said. "They can help you out if you would like them to."

Then, for the first time, she said something that I couldn't get out of my mind. "We will help you. We will pray for you and help you sort out your problems."

That sounded different to my ears. How can a white lady say she will help me? Most of the white people I used to meet hated black people. She was completely different.

She told me about the missionaries and asked if I would like them to help me sort out my life. She made an appointment, and the missionaries came. We talked. They asked what was wrong with my life, but not deeply. I was frank and told them, because I had already told Sister Jenny what was going on.

"Okay, we can help you if you are willing. We will help you pray, and the Lord will help you."

By now, I had a little feeling that there was a Lord. More especially, I looked back at what I went through and how I was saved and protected. I had a feeling my life had been spared. It came to my mind that if I prayed, maybe the Lord would help me.

When I looked at a picture of Joseph Smith, I thought, "What would make me go out like that and do the same thing?" I felt I was being pushed.

One day I went to look for work. I was tired, because I had been looking for work the whole week, all the time. After Monday, Tuesday, and Wednesday went by, I got work. Then I had a feeling that there was something that had helped me find work. The missionaries had helped me pray.

They also asked me to come to the Vereeniging chapel. I came on Saturday, because the company I was working for didn't work on Saturdays. I came with friends and left my wife home, though I told her about my appointment.

When we came to town, something happened to me and my two friends. We bought ourselves beer in cans and some chewing tobacco. They wanted me to leave the appointment and go buy some more liquor. But I said, "No, I must go. I promised."

The other thing that made me go was that I was working with Sister Jenny. If I dropped the appointment, maybe I could not look her in the face.

Something happened with the liquor. I had drunk two cans, but it was just as if I had drunk water. Nothing happened to me.

The missionaries gave me the lessons and asked me to pray in any language. I prayed in Sotho. They asked me if I would like to come to church. I said no, but we would see as the time went by. After the discussion, we departed.

Then I came to church, and it didn't take long before I was baptized. I had to stop smoking and drinking. The missionaries asked me to pray about that. I prayed only twice, and that was that. I found that to stop drinking was a little bit difficult, but it didn't bother me much.

The difference that happened in my life was that after I was baptized, everybody at the chapel seemed to be a friend. The Church members mostly were friends and mothers and fathers to me. I began to feel loved. I felt I was in the right place. All along I had been trying to find a place like this to be loved, but until now I had never been loved. I found that the Church was the right place for me to be.

Even if I was having a quarrel with my wife, we would come by bus and not be talking to each other, but after the meetings, our quarrel would be over.

The happiest thing that came to my life is that I baptized my wife. I didn't know how to say the baptismal prayer, so Brother Snyman said the prayer, and I said the words after him.

Then I began to feel that I was somebody amongst the people. I started to study the gospel, trying to understand it. But because of my low education, the English was a bit difficult for me to understand. Most of the Bible words are a bit difficult in English.

What I do is open to a verse in English, and open to the same verse in my mother language. I compare them and can understand. I am also attending the adult education school.

Everything the missionaries said and did made me happy. Everything they said to me was nice to hear. Also, the way the verses of scripture were taught in my other church was not the same as in this church. They are better explained. I understand the scriptures better.

Baptism was a new life to me. I became a completely new person. Sister Bridge baked a nice big cake for me. Everybody around me was saying, "Congratulations, Isaac." I felt very good, very pleased.

I still sometimes feel a little down on things other than the Church, but I decided to spend more hours with my family than with my friends. There is a big difference. My children understand me better. They know what kind of a person I am, and how I will react to them.

I pray within me that God will help me with my children, that they must not lead the same life that I experienced, because it was really tough. It was bad, and embarrassing. I pray that the Lord will help us and give us strength and better understanding of life, so that we can live life as it comes to us. Especially if we can build our children when they are young, and teach them how to go about their lives, they will build the good life.

I thank God for what he is to me. I thank him for the many blessings he has given me, especially in answering my prayers. I know that God lives, and that Jesus Christ is his Son, and that he loves me. I know that God always looks after us. He loves us and wants us to be as he is.

22

Elias M. Vis, Sr.

A New Life and a New Covenant—Bring Peace and Harmony to Our Land

Elias M. Vis, Sr. made a decision when he was twelve years of age that he would never smoke or drink liquor in any form. Later in life he became a preacher in a Protestant church. Elias was very outspoken and politically active in anti-apartheid movements. Finding the gospel and joining the Church brought great changes into his life and into his home. He was born in 1935 in Brandfordt, Orange Free State, South Africa, and grew up in a family of four children. He and his wife, Alice, were married in 1966 and are the parents of four children.

I am from the Xhosa nationality. My people fought against the English settlers and strayed all over the central part of South Africa. We consider ourselves a great nation, because we fought for our little land and for ourselves. We were instructed in our homes that we should not marry into other tribes. My parents wanted me to marry in my nationality. I told my mother, when she was still alive, that I desired to marry any girl whom I loved, even if she wasn't from my tribe. My mother said that was okay. She died when I was sixteen years old.

My parents worked as laborers on a farm. They were very poor. I was brought up by my grandparents and, when they died, by an aunt.

In 1947 when I was twelve years old, I decided that I would never take liquor and never smoke. My stepfather was a heavy drinker and smoker, and I found that this was not good.

I started work as a herd boy, looking after the cattle and sheep that belonged to a farmer. I used to give the farmer a bad time, because I was much politically minded. I would object to the way he treated us. I would say, "No, not like that. I want it like this." When the farmer would swear at me, I would say, "No, don't swear at me. You must talk to me properly."

I also felt that I was not inferior to the farmers, even though I was just a worker. They used to call us baboons, but I told them they mustn't. They wouldn't be able to run the farms without us, even though we were only young boys of sixteen. We were there to help the farmers, because they by themselves wouldn't be able to do the job we were doing.

The old farmer got cross and told his wife, who told my aunt, "Tell the boy he mustn't talk like that to the boss."

I had a desire for a better life. I had a desire to live like a white man. I had a desire to have a family of my own, and to work hard and make a better living. I didn't want my children to be uneducated. I had all that in my heart.

I had a dream that if I was educated, I would go to parliament, to nations, and make peace amongst them, by telling them that people shouldn't make wars and frictions.

Many farmers didn't like me. They used to say to my aunt, "This son of your sister is a very spoiled child. That is not good."

In 1953 I decided to come to town, because I wanted to become educated, and there were no schools on the farms. That was my biggest worry in life.

Schools were very far away from the farms. My mother had once sent me to a school about seven miles away. I had walked. But I had gone to that school, as a boy of eight or nine, for only one year.

When I was nineteen years old, I enrolled in night school in an adult center, where I continued up to standard six [eighth grade]; thereafter, I joined a correspondence college. Of course, I was on and off with my studies, because of other commitments. I had to work hard to prepare myself for my future family.

I was baptized in the Full Gospels church, then went to the African Gospels church, where I stayed for twenty years. I kept my covenant in that church, though I did not think the church was based on Christianity. My commitment was for personal reasons.

In the church I belonged to, I visited people, especially those who didn't attend church, and also some people in the hospital, until such time that I was inactive. I opposed taking wine as a sacrament, because I didn't drink alcohol. I suggested that we use water, but the church people were very much against it. So I stayed away because of my commitment not to have wine or alcohol, even though the church people liked my preaching on Sundays, especially the young men and women.

I wanted the girl I married to have three qualities: she must not smoke or drink, she must be brilliant, and she must have sympathy. In other words, she must have a backbone. When a person is able to stand problems, you say that person has a backbone. By "brilliant," I mean that she should be able to bring up my children in the correct way.

I broke six engagements before I found the right wife. I wanted to marry only once, marry for life, so that only death could separate us. I've told my wife, Alice, that she mustn't think she will ever be divorced.

One day I prayed and received an answer that breaking engagements is a sin, because it hurts other people. I was told that the girl whom I would choose and marry, Heavenly Father would bring.

When I was twenty-nine years old, I was introduced to Alice. She was eighteen years old and attending school. I saw her and spoke with her, then paid her a visit, to ask her what she wanted to be in the future. I told her the type of girl I wanted. She had all the qualities I was looking for in a wife.

She was from another tribe. Some of my relatives didn't like her at first, but later on they loved her more than some of the other daughters-in-law.

Still, after six months of going with her, I decided I didn't like her anymore. I stayed away from her for three months.

One Saturday evening I had a dream. My late mother came to me from the east as I was sitting on a green lawn. When she came up to me, I said to her, "Here is the girl I love." My mother picked the girl up and said, "This is the daughter-in-law who I have been waiting for." She put her down next to me on my right-hand side.

That dream came again—three times in one night. I woke up in the morning, ready to go to Sunday school. I washed myself and went to Alice, but I didn't tell her the dream.

She asked me where I had been. I said I had missed her a lot. We sat the whole Sunday and discussed our schools and other things.

The next time I came back, I told her I had made my decision. "I want you to consider marriage."

She said she was ready at any time, so we got married.

She has changed my life. She has got a backbone, she has sympathy, she is brilliant.

In many things I was not a soft person. I was the type of man who was very hard. I was once fighting in a political meeting I was attending. My wife is the type of person who tells me, if I clash with another man, to keep cool. "Leave that man alone. Keep your dignity," she says. I force myself to listen to her. My grandfather used to tell me that if you listen to your wife, you will be out of trouble every time.

I love Alice. My relatives love her very much. Her parents love me; they are wonderful. Alice is a nursing sister by profession. Because she liked nursing, I told her to go and train as a nurse. She trained six and one-half years, while I stayed with our two children. She was working in Pelonomi Hospital when our last child, Nomfesane (which means "mercy" in English), was born. I believe that our Heavenly Father had mercy on us.

Only now am I turning soft through reading the standard works of the Church. I have changed now. My wife even says that I have changed in the seven years we have been in the Church.

In 1970 a member of the Church, a secretary in the driving school where I was employed, told me about the Church, though I had seen the church building before. It is just a few buildings away from us. She said it was a chapel, but I didn't think it looked like a chapel. It was not built like other churches. She also told me about the Book of Mormon. I said, "We believe in the Bible."

One day we found an invitation in our post box to go to the Bloemfontein Hotel at seven o'clock, to see a film to be shown by the missionaries. Alice worked until seven in the evening, so I waited for her. We were the last couple to arrive. The hall was full.

The film was *Man's Search for Happiness*. After the film everyone wrote their names in a book. Some of our neighbors were there too. Three days later, I was invited to meet Brother Corrigan, the mission leader in the branch. I said to my wife, "I am not going there. I don't believe these people. Do you think they will sit at a table and eat with us?"

I want to say that there is a great difference between the way the members of the Church live and the way other people live. Many of my white friends would say we must pay them a visit, and when we did we would sit in the garage and they would bring us tea, but not in *their* cups.

Alice said to me, "You must go meet Brother Corrigan first. Then you can see if these people are the same."

To my surprise, I sat at the table and drank herbal tea with them. I found that Sister Corrigan's mother had worked with me in the driving school, when Sister Corrigan was a little girl. I was welcomed in their home.

I came home and told my wife that I had met different people. Religion could make a difference.

I was visited by the missionaries, but I didn't like them. I liked their teaching, but I didn't like it when they came to my house. When I saw them, I hid myself. Then my wife would come and say, "The missionaries were here. They were giving us very nice teachings."

When they did find me, I would sit down and listen to them and ask questions. Some of the questions were political.

I don't know why I didn't like them. I had a feeling that they came only because they wanted us to come to their church, and not because they cared about us. But it was not so. I was misjudging them.

I have found that there is no difference in members of The Church of Jesus Christ of Latter-day Saints. You can go to Cape Town, to Durban, to Johannesburg, and the members are all the same. They are good examples.

When I asked a political question, one missionary said, "I am not a politician, you know." My wife counseled me. "No, no," she said, "you must ask questions according to what *they* talk to you about. These missionaries are bringing religion to us. You must ask them questions about the Book of Mormon and what they have told us." Alice is brilliant.

One holiday I forgot that the missionaries said they would come, and just as I was about to leave, I looked out of the window and saw the missionaries' car stopping in front of my house. "Here are these young men again," I told Alice. "You must tell them I'm not here."

"No way," she said. "I am going to tell them you are hiding yourself in your room. I am tired of your hiding."

So I sat down and asked questions.

"How about joining the Church?" they asked.

"Yes," I told them. "I feel that I can join your church."

My wife doubted, because we had a new minister in our church. "What will he say?"

I said to her in my language, "I feel sorry for the way I've treated these two young men. As far as I have investigated their church and the members there, I feel we should join them. Forget the minister."

So I promised the missionaries that I would join, and they taught me and my wife.

We were baptized on 27 June 1981. Two of our children, Emily and Elias Junior, were also taught by the missionaries. Both have been through four years of seminary, and Elias is now on a mission in England.

What impressed me most about the Church were the teachings of Joseph Smith, his visions of Heavenly Father and Jesus, and his vision of Moroni. These impressed me because visions are similar to dreams. I used to have such things, and I believe in them.

Joseph Smith was told to join none of the existing churches; Jesus would organize His church. Most of the churches in South Africa belong to people, such that if the father dies, the son will take over the leadership. The administration of The Church of Jesus Christ of Latter-day Saints is far different. When I asked about prophets, the roles of the prophets, Apostles, seventies, and bishops were explained to me. The Church doesn't have a paid ministry, but I found it works very smoothly.

I read in the Book of Mormon that I must pray and ask if the teachings of the book were true. I did, and the truth of them was revealed to me. Before I met the Church, I prayed, and it came to me that there was a true church of Jesus Christ on earth, but I was not told which church it was. When I found these teachings, I knew I had found the church I had been looking for. It also suited my wife. She believes in it very much.

Another time I prayed, and it came to me that there was a church which is good, and that the head of that church was Jesus. This I saw in what I call a dream. I distinguish between dreams and visions. A dream comes to you in your sleep. A vision is what is revealed to you when you pray—as when I prayed to get a good wife, and my mother came to me.

So I had no difficulty believing in Joseph Smith's visions. He was in a room, it became light, he saw a personage (Moroni), and he described the personage. The same thing happened when Joseph Smith was baptized and when he received the Melchizedek Priesthood.

I doubted the Book of Mormon at first, but when I was taught about it and read about it, I learned that it was a second witness of Jesus Christ. When I read it, I felt that it was written by people who were given revelation. It is not the minds of men who wrote the book, but the Holy Ghost, who filled these men. The writers were prompted to include things which they saw, or things which they heard from other people, or things that were put in their minds.

I find that the Book of Mormon gives each and every nation its place. It is unlike an ordinary history book, which will contain a lot of untrue statements. When a historian writes a book, he will do it to suit his nation. The Book of Mormon is not like this. It is a clear book. Everyone can feel at home with it.

When I was baptized into the Lord's church, I felt a change. I felt a new life and a new covenant. I was happy, because I felt that everything I had desired had come. I found everything in the Church, especially the way we do the sacrament, to be the way I had thought it should be years ago, although I hadn't been a member and hadn't lived some of the commandments taught by the gospel.

The commandment that impressed me most was the law of chastity. I was to have only one wife. I was to live clean and love my family and have family home evening. I was to study the standard works of the Church. Also, I had no difficulty accepting the Word of Wisdom.

I had difficulty only in my political beliefs. Politics are different than religion. You see politics in different ways, depending on the situation in a certain place.

As a boy of nineteen, I joined the African National Congress (ANC), before it was banned and its leaders skipped the country. I knew the leaders of that party, and they inspired us. I loved it very much. I took part in civic matters.

The result of my joining the Church is that I've decided to give up politics, stay in the Church, and do more work for the Church, more work for the Lord in a Christian way, because I have found that the state government and the divine government don't have to clash. The South African government likes people to be religious. That is why you find so many churches in the country. Concerning religion, the South African government doesn't disturb people. So I find it easy for me to leave politics and stay in religion. Doing both would contradict my way of life. In politics there are many ways to do things. If I stay involved in the Church, it gives me a chance to practice more religion, to be more righteous, to talk to people more freely, to help bring all nations together, to teach more people the right way, and to bring peace and harmony to our land.

In 1985 I was consulted by a young man who remembered that I was a member of the ANC. He said he had been told by his leaders about me and the role I played in politics. They asked him to come to me and choose me as an adviser in the United States Democratic Front, a wing of the ANC. I told him that because of my personal religious beliefs, I didn't think I would ever fit in with that group. It didn't suit me anymore. The leaders of that group could form their government. I would work to help form a divine government. I would bring the gospel to people.

I wanted to help my political friends by teaching them the gospel. We talked for five hours. I told them about the Church. I told them I could always come and pray for them. I went to one of them once and gave him a blessing, and he recovered. He said to me, "That is a good role you are playing, but we want you to be a leader."

"I am a man of religion now," I said. "I am different."

They accepted that, because they believe that they also need religious people in their government.

I don't like racists. I must love everybody, because I must teach the gospel to everybody. I must love black, white, yellow, and so on, regardless of color. I must not say that a nation is purposely trying to hurt us, or is discriminating against us. They don't know what they are doing. I must teach them. When a white man becomes a member of the Church, he has to give up discrimination. Why can't I do it too?

When I joined the Church, many of my family were very angry. They asked me how I felt amongst whites. "Do you feel at home?"

"Oh, yes, I feel very much at home. You must come."

Many people used to come and visit me. They would tell me I must stay in a church that is only black. But that is discrimination. If I was to stay in a church that is only black, that is not the Church of Jesus Christ; that is a church of black people. The Church of Jesus Christ of Latter-day Saints includes everybody.

My friends from the other churches have given up on me.

I told my uncle in Lesotho that my son was going on a mission to England. He was very happy. He said, "I am a minister, and I have never been to England. I am happy that your son is going on a mission." He praised that and said the Church was good. I told him he must come and join the Church.

I am preparing myself and my wife to go on a mission when we retire; and my little daughter also says she wants to go on a mission when she grows up.

I believe that Heavenly Father has brought me into the Church. The changes in me have been great. I used to be a man of revenge — if you hit me with a brick, I wanted to hit you twice. Many people who were enemies to me, I have tried to make good friends. Many people whom I wanted to punish (and some I had already punished), I have come to be friends with. Those I didn't punish before I joined the Church have escaped the punishment. Those I had already punished, I tried to heal. I spoke to them, and they feel they won't have my punishment anymore.

I have learned to trust and respect other people. I have learned not to judge other people according to their deeds. If a person is wrong, I must show them the right way. It is my duty to teach them.

I called my children to me and told them I no longer wanted to beat them with my *sambok* when they were naughty. I didn't feel happy when I punished them. Now we just talk. We spend a lot of time in family home evening talking over our differences. I show them and teach them; I want them to feel at home. They mustn't fear me, but feel they can come to their parents with their problems.

In November of 1980 I said to my wife, "Dear, I've got a feeling that in the future we shall sit at a table with white people in this country. As of now, I want you to lay the table for us each and every time. We must teach these children to use the knife and fork to eat with. We must teach them table manners, because I've got a feeling that very soon we shall eat and drink tea with whites."

Soon after, I was invited with my family to the Corrigans' home, where we sat at the table and ate. I was also invited by President Osmond to eat with him. I was invited by the elders to join their table. At a conference in Johannesburg, I sat with whites—and so on. We are now "westernized." What I was saying to my wife was correct.

Since I have joined the Church, I no longer feel guilty. I have learned to forgive myself. I also feel more protected in life, such that wherever I go and wherever I am, I remember that feeling. I don't fear anything. I don't even fear to die, as long as it isn't negligently —for nonsense. I am very careful in life, and that is why I don't fear.

In my patriarchal blessing I am told that I will be a bridge for my people to come to the gospel. I was happy to learn that I am a descendant of Ephraim by adoption. I really feel blessed to be among the children of God, and a member of the tribe chosen from the chosen. I don't know how to describe it—it is just a great experience.

One time, long before I joined the Church, I dreamt I was in a house, in white clothes. The house was unusual to me. I saw I was wearing white with my family. The meaning of the dream didn't come clear to me. Now it is clear to me that the house was the temple. Temple work is very sacred; it is our Heavenly Father's work, given to us.

In the temple, I felt I was in another world, a world of peace, of happiness. I felt a sense of eternity, as if I would be there the rest of my life. When my family was sealed to me, it was as if all the teachings I had received had prepared us. It was a new experience, something I had never had before.

I feel that my family is mine for eternity. I hope this can happen to everybody. If they join the Church, it can happen.

I advise all my posterity to be members of The Church of Jesus Christ of Latter-day Saints, to believe in our Savior, and to serve the Lord. I would like all my grandchildren to live righteously and follow their grandfather's life. I would like them to read the standard works, and to be honest with themselves and with their community. Each should serve a mission. Each should follow the prophet's revelations, because we live best if we follow our prophet's guidance.

I bear my testimony to all, that the Church is true. I sustain all my Church leaders. Joseph Smith was indeed a prophet of Jesus, our Savior. He translated the Book of Mormon for the benefit of all nationalities. I have prayed about that book, and have been told that it and the Church are true. The Book of Mormon is a second witness of Christ.

23

Ella Volenhoven

Now I Realize...
What I Am Worth

Ella Volenhoven, born in 1938 in Robertson, Cape, South Africa, experienced a most tragic upbringing as a young girl. She was compelled to work almost as a slave to the white family who reared her. Only through the intervention of the missionaries and gospel teachings was she able to escape and overcome the painful effects of the past. Ella joined the Church in 1975, has since been to Salt Lake City, where she received her temple ordinances, and has served as a worker in the temple in Johannesburg, South Africa. Hers is a marvelous story of courage, faith, and forgiveness.

I was raised by a white family. My mother was a domestic servant for them, and I was born when she was very young. She was not married when I was born, and when I was eight days old, I was given away to the white family, who raised me and with whom I lived for most of my childhood and grown-up life. Although my mother worked for the family, she never touched me to dress or bathe me. The white woman did that.

When I was six or seven years old, my mother left, and I had to continue on with the family. Till this day I haven't seen my real father. Whether he is colored or black or white, I don't know. I have seen my mother a few times, and I know that she is a colored woman.

I grew very close to the family and loved them very much. I couldn't ask for better parents. If I had to choose, I would have chosen them, because they were the most wonderful parents I could have had. They were very kind to me, even through all the hardships I was made to suffer. There were many times when I got hidings [physical punishment], but I am glad for those. They helped make me a better person. When I became older, I was able to join the Church as the person I was, with no bad faults or things I had done which I should feel sorry for. The family had two daughters.

I never had the opportunity to go to school, because I was told by the family that I needed to repay them for what they were doing for me. I was never allowed to mix with my own race; I was always amongst white people. I was not allowed to go to a colored church. I was not allowed to speak to a man, because the family thought I might run away with him. I was never allowed to associate with anybody else.

I had to make my own clothing or recycle old clothing for myself. I had only pocket money. I never earned a salary which I could use to go into a store and buy something. I was twenty-three or twenty-four before I had my first pair of shoes to wear—and those were handed over to me by someone else. Because they were too big, I had to put newspaper in the toes so that I could wear them. I was allowed to wear them only on Sundays. Before that, I had to walk barefoot, even through the South African winters, even when I was a grown-up.

I was brought up as a prisoner amongst white people. I don't say this to degrade the whites; this is just the way I was brought up. If I don't tell things as they were, nobody will understand that in these times, a person can still live under circumstances like mine.

Even though I was brought up amongst white people, I was always told I was not part of them, but colored, and that I needed to know my place. That was very hard, because there are times when you want to be amongst your own people, but you can't be, because of your position.

When my mother left, my hardships in life started. When I was eight or nine years old, I had to garden, clean the house, cook, wash, and iron. I worked from six in the morning until eleven thirty at night, seven days a week. Also, I am a tiny woman, only four feet nine inches tall. Because I was so small, I had to stand on a wooden box to reach the table to iron. In those days we did not have electric appliances. We had the old irons that we heated up on the stove. Also, everything had to be washed by hand, because there were no washing machines.

The washing was put in water to soak on Sunday night, and

early Monday morning (and sometimes on other days too) I had to wash my feet, then step on the washing to get it clean. Then I would let the dirty water run out and put clean water in and rewash the clothes. And it was not hot water, but icy cold water out of a tap.

I can remember hanging wash up during the Cape winters, when it was so cold outside that when I would turn around the clothes would be frozen stiff on the line. I was barefoot; my feet cracked, with blood running out of them.

Those were the circumstances under which I had to work. Not having an education, I didn't realize there could be better things in life. I was always told that nobody else would take me, because I had no education. I must stay where I was. So I was held a prisoner, but I didn't know it.

It was only when I met the Mormon missionaries that I realized my life could be changed. But I was too scared to change my life, because I had always been told I could never be a success in life, only a failure.

When my white mother died in 1961, I was twenty-two years old; I realized that I was not going to have a mother anymore. I couldn't understand why I had to lose two mothers—my physical mother, and my adopted mother. I stayed on in the home to look after my father, because I had promised my mother that I would look after him. From then on, the real unhappiness in my life began.

One of the daughters hated me very much. She came with her husband and son to live with her father, because the laws of the country said that I as a colored girl could not live with only one white man in the home. So the other family moved in so that I could continue with the family and run the home for them.

I began to have to get up earlier than before, at five o'clock. In the morning when I washed, there would be only ice cold water; I was not allowed to take hot-water baths. I had to wait on the daughter like a nurse, till she left for work. My father, now in his eighties, was like a small child; he couldn't do anything for himself. After the daughter and her husband left for work, I had to look after their son. I worked very hard, and it was very difficult.

The worst thing was that the daughter hit me—with her hand or with anything she could pick up. Her husband had to keep quiet, because she ruled him, and she ruled me. I just kept quiet all the time. This continued for thirteen years.

Then, in 1974 the Mormon missionaries moved in, and they started to tell me I couldn't live like that. "Your Heavenly Father doesn't want you to live like this," they would say. But I was too scared even to talk. Because I didn't have any education, I didn't know what might happen to me.

Things got even much worse, but I still would not do what the missionaries advised me to do.

My half brother tried to get me to leave, but I begged him and his wife to leave me alone, and never contact me. That made him very angry.

Things got so bad, and with the missionaries begging me to go away, I realized that there could be something better than the circumstances under which I was living. Two times I even tried to take my own life, but the missionaries took me to the hospital and saved my life. I thought I had been such a bad person, as the daughter always told me. The missionaries told her what I had tried to do and that she needed to change her attitude toward me. That was the worst thing they could have done, because then she beat me more. She told me that if I had killed myself it would have been better for her, that she wouldn't have even gone to the trouble to bury me, but would have just let me dry and rot. The missionaries had said they could no longer live in a house where there was so much fighting and shouting.

One Monday morning, after the family went to work, the missionaries talked to me for three hours solid, continuously telling me that I could no longer stay there. I cried and begged them to leave me. They said, "Pray to your Heavenly Father to help you." I was in such a state that I didn't believe there could be a change in my life. "What's the use of praying?" I said. "My Heavenly Father doesn't love me anymore. If he loved me, he wouldn't let me be punished like I am today!"

They went ahead and prayed for me, and eventually I got onto my knees, because the Spirit was so strongly present in the room that morning. I asked my Heavenly Father to show me what to do with my life, and to help me. That was the first time I had earnestly begged my Heavenly Father to give me guidance and help.

At this time, the turning point in my life came.

Twenty-four hours after I prayed, I had a telephone call from the mission president, inviting me to come up and work in the mission home. I told him I couldn't do that; I had promised that I would look after my father until he died. He asked me, "If your mother were alive today, would she want you to be living under the circumstances you are living under now?"

I told him no.

"Then you have no need to stay anymore. You have paid the family back more than enough for what they have done for you.

You are a grown woman. You are no longer a child. Your father has daughters, and he is no longer your responsibility."

He said he would phone back later in the week for an answer, and in the meantime I needed to go to my knees and pray and fast about the decision.

I accused one of the missionaries of talking to the mission president and arranging for the job, but he denied it. "Don't you see that your Heavenly Father has answered your prayer? He has prepared a way to help you."

The shock was so severe that I burst into tears, realizing that my Heavenly Father really had answered my prayer. When I calmed down, I turned to the missionaries and asked, "What do I do?"

They told me the decision was mine from there on.

The next morning I again asked them what I should do. They said they were not going to influence me. I needed to make the decision myself.

That is when I realized that I was a grown-up woman and needed to make my own decisions.

The daughter continued beating me all the time. The worst beating was the day she grabbed a bread knife and tried to stab me with it. Still frightened, I went down to the police station and said I would like to speak to one of the policemen. (Most of the policemen knew my father.) "What is wrong with you, Ella?" the policeman asked. My face was cut and bruised from a beating the previous Saturday.

He wanted to bring charges against the family, but I told him, "I don't want that. All I want is my freedom to go and not be arrested."

"You will not be arrested," he promised me. He also advised me not to talk to anyone else about my decision.

I came back to the house and tried to talk to the elders, but they wouldn't listen to me. "You need to make the decision yourself," they said.

When the mission president phoned back, I told him I would start work in the mission home, but I had no money for a train ticket. He said he would pay for the ticket, but I was not to tell anybody where I was going or what I was doing.

That was the hardest thing I ever had to do in my life—to prepare myself to go, leaving my father behind, and not tell anybody. Also, I had never been out of the Cape or been anywhere by myself. The two weeks before I left were the hardest in my life.

The whole afternoon before I left, I cleaned the house and took care of my father. I cried bitterly nearly all the time, not because I was leaving that place, but because I was leaving my father, whom

I loved so much. Later in the evening, after I had put the family to bed, I took the train to come up to the Transvaal. I was so upset that I did not sleep that night on the train, or the following day.

It was six months before the family found me. Even my own brother didn't know where I was. The family accused me of letting my father down and said I was needed, that I should go back and help him.

But I had made the break, and I did not go back. I did go see my father, when he was in a rest home. He was so senile and fragile, he recognized me only very vaguely. I cried much that day.

Several months later I got a phone call from the younger daughter, who was my friend. Her father had passed away. The most upsetting news was that I was not to come down for the funeral.

She told me that before he died he sat up in his bed in full consciousness and asked her if she knew where I was. She told him she did. He told her to tell me that he loved me very much, like one of his own daughters; and he never held it against me that I had left. His hands had been tied, so that he could do nothing for me. He forgave me and hoped he would see me in the next life. He would be waiting for me with his wife, so that I could be part of his family, as I had been before.

On those words, he passed away.

She said she needed to tell me that, so that I should be happy, and not feel that I had let him down.

For the first time in my whole life, I found peace with myself, knowing I had done the right thing.

I have wanted badly to do the temple work for this couple, but I cannot get permission from the family. Those parents come to me regularly in various dreams and just look at me. I know what they want, but there is no way I can do it.

I worked in the mission home for just over a year.

After that, I worked for Woolworth's Pty. Ltd., a large company in South Africa. I worked myself up from assistant cook to the position of canteen supervisor, with eight girls under me.

Then I took a one-year break and went to live in America.

Upon my return to South Africa, I went back to Woolworth's; then, in November of 1987, I began to work at the Johannesburg Temple, as a laundry clerk. I am very proud to work in the Lord's house for him.

I did not meet my brother until I was about twelve or thirteen years old. A young child knocked at the front door. My white mother came and told me my brother was there. I wasn't aware that I had a brother.

My mother was also at the door. As she stepped forward, I flung my arms around her, but she pushed me away, saying, "Don't claim me as your mother. I have just brought your brother to see you, because I had told him about you."

I was allowed to speak to him, and afterwards he phoned me from time to time

I always asked my brother about my mother, because I knew he was in contact with her. I wanted to make peace with her, because after I joined the Church, I felt I needed to do that.

One night my brother told me that my mother did not live far from him. I begged him to take me to go and see her, even though he told me she didn't want to see me. "It will make her very upset and spoil you and her."

But I wanted to see her, so on Sunday we got dressed and went to her place. It was the most unhappy experience of my life. My brother went in first and told her I wanted to see her. She told him that under no circumstances did she want to talk to me, or even see me. The Spirit was so strong at that time that I felt I needed to go in, so I forced myself in.

When I went in, her husband walked out, leaving the two of us alone. It was like I was in a total stranger's house. She looked at me, and I looked at her. I couldn't speak. I was like someone who had completely lost her voice.

For a solid ten minutes, we just stared at each other. I knew she was my mother, the one who gave birth to me.

She asked me what I wanted.

I told her I had missed her all these years, and would love to have contact with her.

She said that the day she gave me away was the day she said she had never had a child, and she never, ever wanted to see me again. Would I please leave immediately.

I left, very upset.

A week later, she arrived at my brother's place, knowing that I was there. She told me she had been worrying the whole week that she had treated me very badly, and that I had done what any daughter would have done.

I put my arms around her and hugged her and cried. It was then, for the first time, that I realized how much I loved and cared for her.

Suddenly she turned funny and pushed me away. She said she just wanted to tell me that, and now needed to go.

My sister-in-law came into the room at that point and said, "What is happening between Mommy and you? This is the first time I have seen her like this."

"I don't know," I said.

That night at the airport, before I flew back to Johannesburg, I was surprised to see my mother in the crowd of those who had come to see loved ones off. When I started to walk toward her, she disappeared in the crowd, and I never saw her again.

I hope to look her up again and try to make peace with her, and tell her that I don't blame her for what she did, because probably I would have done the very same thing, if I was only seventeen years old and had a baby. I also hope to learn who my father is, so that I can get complete peace of mind. Sometimes I feel I have that peace, but sometimes I don't. I think every daughter wants to know what her mother and father look like. I pray that my Heavenly Father will soften my mother's heart.

I still have contact with one daughter of the family I lived with. She and her family stayed with me in my home for a week. They slept and ate in my house, and I took them around and showed them the Transvaal. I hope to spend more time with them.

I also go from time to time on holiday to see the sister who was so mean to me. She has had a stroke and is paralyzed. I believe that to be a Christian, I have to forgive, realizing that she was a sickly woman, and that is why she did what she did. Because she lives in a nursing home and can't do anything for herself, she has asked me to come and look after her. Of course I can't do that, not because I am selfish, but I feel I need to do the best I can with my own life. I look forward to seeing her, because I feel that we need to be together. After all, she is my stepsister, even if she doesn't acknowledge it. These are the only family I really know in life, other than my brother.

I, of course, met the missionaries when they lived at the house where I worked. They took their meals there and started to tell me about the gospel.

Two of the elders, being Americans, couldn't speak Afrikaans. After a couple of months, they came to me and said, "We'll make a deal with you. We will spend an hour a day teaching you English, if you will teach us Afrikaans for an hour a day." That we did. They taught me the English I know.

This deal continued with the next missionaries. One day they were in the lounge having a discussion, and I took my stuff and walked out. "Why don't you stay and listen," they asked.

"I'm not interested in your church," I told them.

But when I started to wash the outside of the house, I asked myself, "Why did I do that? There would be no harm in just carrying on with my work and listening."

The next morning I went to them and said, "When you have a discussion, I would like to just listen, to see what it is about." Still I was not interested at all in their church. I had been told so many things, that I only wanted to stay in one religion.

I listened some more, and then the missionaries asked me if I would like to have some of the discussions. I was scared. "No," I said. "I can't, because the madam wouldn't allow me."

"It can't do any harm to sit down," they said, so I did.

Without Madam knowing, I had the first two discussions, and I started to become interested in the Church.

They taught me many more lessons and asked if I would like to go to their church. I explained that I was not allowed to go to any different church. I was sometimes allowed to go see my brother for an hour, so it was arranged for me to to around the corner and be picked up to go to church.

I did this until one day Madam found out where I was going. I got a big hiding for lying and for going to a different church. The elders were told they were to have no conversations with me. I told them that under no circumstances could I be baptized, because Madam wouldn't allow it.

One elder confronted her, and that was a mistake. I got another hiding. She told me many bad things about the Church.

I did go to a special fireside at the Mowbray Chapel, near Cape Town, which was packed full of Latter-day Saints. The person coming from America that evening for the fireside was Brother Thomas S. Monson, who was touring the mission with the mission president, whom I also met for the first time.

I was very impressed with the fireside, and afterwards the missionaries took me to Brother Monson and introduced him to me. They told him that I might be the first colored lady in the Church in all of South Africa. Everybody knows how big he is, and I have said how small I am. He put his arms around me and gave me a big hug, saying to me, "I know that you will go far in the Church." He told me that I was a very beautiful daughter of my Heavenly Father, who loved me very much and was mindful of my needs.

At that time, I didn't even know that I was going to join the Church, or what was going to happen with my life. The Spirit was so strong that I was in tears.

I returned home that evening and made my bed under the kitchen table, where I usually slept. Madam was furious. "Are you going to join the Mormons!"

On the spur of the moment, I said, "Yes, I am going to join the Mormons."

"Then in that case, you get out of my house now. I don't want you any longer in my house."

I had not yet undressed, so I folded up my bed, went to the back room, and proceeded to pack my clothing. Where I was going at eleven thirty at night, I did not know, but I was determined to leave.

Then she came back in and said she was sorry. She didn't mean what she had said, and I mustn't go. What would happen to her father?

I went back and got into bed.

When the missionaries came home, I was crying, and I told them what had happened.

"Do you realize what is happening to you?" one of them asked.

"No, I don't."

"You are starting to see that you can have a better life."

Madam started watching me, and I was not allowed to be out of her sight or to be anywhere near the missionaries.

I did continue to go to church, without her knowing. From that day on, I also started paying tithing on the little bit of pocket money I got—only forty or sixty cents. But it was my tithing. I promised the elders that I would join the Church, but I wouldn't be in that house when I joined. I would be gone.

I came to work in the mission home in 1975; I was baptized then, when I was thirty-six years old. The day of my baptism was the happiest day of my life.

I can still remember the joy of it. The baptismal chapel is very small, but it was packed that day, because I was the first colored to be baptized into the Church in the Johannesburg area. (I think a colored lady in Cape Town joined before I did.) For a long time, I was the only colored in the Church in Johannesburg, and that made me live a higher standard, because everybody, even the whites, was looking at me to be an example.

I was working in the mission home when the announcement came that coloreds and blacks could hold the priesthood. The mission president's wife, Sister LeBaron, came to the kitchen and told me. I cannot describe the joy it brought into my life that day. We hugged each other and I cried my heart out. I knew that I was not going to be the only colored one at church anymore.

I don't remember much of what the missionaries first taught me, only that we return to our Heavenly Father and live in his presence with all our loved ones around us. The lesson on the plan of salvation impressed me the most.

The missionaries also gave me the best example of the way to live. They were fine, clean gentlemen. The more I am in the Church, the more I want to be like them. I hope that I will be the means, one day, of bringing many of my people and generation into the Church, by being an example to them. The Church is a beautiful organization, a lovely brotherhood and sisterhood.

I know that my Heavenly Father has a plan for me. What it is, I do not know. I live from day to day to find out what his plan is. I think part of the plan was to build a temple in South Africa so that I could come and work in it. I can see that I needed to go to America and have that experience, then come back to South Africa to work in the Lord's house. I would be needed more in my own country, amongst my own people.

After I received my patriarchal blessing and realized what was in it, I took it back to the patriarch and told him it was someone else's blessing, because it was not meant for me. The patriarch told me it was my blessing, given by my Heavenly Father. It said what the Lord wanted me to be. I am happy to have it as a guide in my life.

When I was in the mission home, I went to various classes, to learn to read and write a little bit. Every day I had an hour lesson, and in my last six months there, I was very surprised with myself, the way I had gained the knowledge to be able to read and write. My Heavenly Father has given me a wonderful memory so I can memorize things. I am grateful for this ability.

I sing in the ward and stake choirs, and everybody is amazed that I can sing along and yet not be able to read. The minute I hear the music, I can memorize the words and sing with no problem.

In 1986 I took my endowment out in the Provo Temple. All I can remember is that I was very emotional. I cried through the whole session. The first missionary I ever met, David Hirsche, was there with his wife, Pam, and his mother and father. In the celestial room afterwards, David told me this was the happiest day of his life, to be able to be part of my going through the temple. They took me out to lunch afterwards in the temple cafeteria.

There was another black person in the session, and he came up and congratulated me. He said that he himself had just gone through for the first time. I was very happy to see that someone else had taken the same steps as I had taken that day.

David and Pam then drove me to the town where David's former missionary companion worked. I just walked into his shop and said to him, "I would like to buy a washing machine."

He looked at me, then flung his arms around me. He recognized me straightaway. When we told him what we had just done, he burst out in tears, he was so happy and glad to see me. And I was happy to see him.

I later went to the Salt Lake Temple, and during my stay in Salt Lake City, I went to the temple every week.

One night when I was sitting in the foyer after a session, suddenly a man walked up to me and said, "Hello, Ella. How are you?"

It was a missionary who had served in South Africa who hadn't seen me for six years or longer, but he recognized me immediately. The day he left South Africa, I wasn't home, so he wrote on a card, "If I don't see you in this life, I will see you in the next." He was very surprised to see me sitting in the Salt Lake Temple. It was a happy meeting.

I am very grateful every day when I wake up that I can come to the Lord's house and serve him. This is a most enjoyable and happy place to work.

I have grown greatly over the last thirteen or so years. How much more experience I have gained, and what a better person it has made me! Not that I wasn't a good person before I joined the Church, but now I realize what my potential is in life, and what I am worth. I am sorry I didn't come in contact with the Church before, when I was much younger, so I would have more experience in the Church. I might have met someone and married. My patriarchal blessing tells me that I will meet someone someday who will take me to the Lord's house. I know that the Lord will send that person on my path one day.

I went through very bitter times, and I can see today why I had to go through those hardships—to make me the person I am today.

Even with all this country's problems, there are happy times you can have here. Whoever reads my story, let me counsel them not to leave their country for a different country. Stay where you are, even if there are problems. You know what you have in your own country, but you don't know what you are going to have in another country. I tried leaving, and I realized that my home was still my home, and where I needed to be.

I hope that if my family—my nieces or some of their children, or an aunt or uncle—read this, they will realize what an example I have tried to be and what I have gone through. I hope that they will never give away a child, so that someone has to go through the pain and hardship of never having a family. Even though I grew up with a family, I was still not a part of that family. I still see myself as an outsider today.

I would be very happy to be the instrument to bring my brother into the Church. He would be a most wonderful priesthood holder in the gospel, and would bring his family in. I pray for him every day, and even though he does not want me to discuss the Church with him, I know that one day someone will knock on his door and he will, by having seen my example, come into the Church.

My work in the temple is but a preparation for a proselyting mission for the Church—what I will do later in life when I have enough experience to become an instrument to bring the gospel to my people and my nation. That will be the happiest joy in my life. At the moment, there are not many coloreds in the Church, because of their traditions and their religions. I don't condemn other churches. They have their religion and their rights. But it is up to every one individually to find out what salvation is, and to do what is prepared for that individual to do in life.

I know that this church is true, and I am very grateful to be a member of it in this dispensation. I am also grateful to be of the tribe of Ephraim, and I try to live up to the responsibility that has been put on my shoulders from the day I joined the Church, because everyone looks to me as an example. Wherever I go in life, people say I am different. When I tell them I am a Mormon, they say, "Oh, I can see why you are different." It is a high responsibility to always do the right things and to live the standards of the Church.

Africa